TWO MEN AND THEIR MONSTER

Two Men and Their Monster

Harry Low built a Walkerville legend.
Vern Myslichuk raised it from the dead.

Gary May

Your Story Publishing
2015

ISBN 978-0-9867534-6-6

Cataloguing in Publication data available from Library and Archives Canada.

Cover photo: Devonshire Lodge photo from 1928, courtesy Jim Cooper.
Back cover: Winter view of back of house from 1950.
Photos are provided by Vern Myslichuk or Gary May, unless otherwise indicated.

Researched and written by Gary May, Windsor, Ontario, Canada
Design and layout: Karen Veryle Monck, Benchmark Publishing & Design Inc., Windsor, Ontario, Canada
Editing: Linda Mondoux, Windsor, Ontario, Canada

Your Story Publishing, 203 – 2175 Wyandotte Street East, Windsor, Ontario, Canada, N8Y 5B9
Telephone: 519-258-2222
www.garymay.ca

Printed by Ball Media Corporation, Brantford, Ontario, Canada
Printed and bound in Canada

This book is dedicated to the staff of BetterMade Cabinets, whose knowledge and efforts were critical in bringing Harry Low's house back to life. They stood by me, never wavering from the big picture, never ceasing to believe in our ability to restore this magnificent home. Through hours of planning, designing and back-breaking work in the relentless heat of summer, they pushed on, every one of them a hero – a rock star.

Vern Myslichuk

Harry Low imagined Devonshire Lodge.
He lived there from 1928 to 1934.

Vern Myslichuk purchased the house in 2012,
restored it and moved in in 2014.

Table of contents

Devonshire Lodge, 2021 Ontario Street. Its original address was 288 Devonshire Road, Walkerville. (Joe Acton)

Chapter 1:

The House That Roared

CAN A HOUSE POSSESS ATTITUDE? IF IT can, it's hard to imagine one with more attitude than the house that dominates the corner of Ontario Street and Devonshire Road in Windsor's Walkerville precinct. Christened Devonshire Lodge by its creator, notorious 1920s rumrunner Harry Low, the house stands brash, assertive, saucy, arrogant – a reflection of the man's own character. There is swagger in the manner in which it straddles its territory and confronts its neighbours. Again, like Harry Low himself.

Devonshire Lodge was built in dismissive defiance of the notion that a house should sit square to its street; instead, it stands insolently at a jaunty angle.

Its imposing rough-cut stone walls once earned it the cheeky nickname "Harry's rockpile." Its curved façade denotes forcefulness. Its wavy, faux-Cotswold cottage roofline imitates a rolling sea. Its leaded glass windows infuse the interior light with a mystical aura. Its recessed balcony guards the entranceway in a medieval manner. It defies definition. Ultimately, it laughs at those who struggle to categorize its style; there is no style, merely an assemblage of characteristics that caught Harry Low's fancy.

It is a house that was built to roar: Look at me!

It surely roared at the current owner, Vern Myslichuk, when a chance shortcut through the historic neighbourhood took him past its hulking form. After he bought and restored it, Myslichuk, founder and owner of BetterMade Cabinets, affectionately dubbed his house "the monster."

In Old Walkerville, a neighbourhood that is known for its grand and elegant homes – sturdy Tudors and decorative examples of the Arts and Crafts style – this house stands apart. The castle-like Willistead Manor has long since passed from private hands to the city's ownership, while the fabled Cooper Court was torn down decades ago, leaving Devonshire Lodge without peer among Walkerville's private residences. In fact, many say there is nothing to match it among private homes anywhere in Southwestern Ontario.

It is a striking, boastful memorial to the man who imagined it, a man born of humble beginnings who successfully circumnavigated Canada's byzantine laws governing alcohol manufacture and sale during the

Roaring Twenties. Because he could afford it, Harry Low paid a spectacular price to build this house after rising to the lofty heights of his trade in the era of Flappers and Gatsby, of rumrunning, smuggling, ransom-fuelled kidnappings and murders. His life was touched by each.

His untimely fall was as spectacular, and even quicker, than his rise.

You could call him reckless, but never lacking in drive or genius. Even after he stumbled, he never gave up, never stopped looking for the next best thing. He must have been heartbroken to lose his beloved home. Did he ever pass it by afterward and stop to wonder: What if?

Low's story reflects the arrival and fading away of a brief period in history that Windsor/Essex residents have only recently come to appreciate and embrace with fascination. This "monster" house is a product of, and stands as a reminder of that time when government's determination to force a set of moral principles on the people led to widespread and shameless disregard for the law and created a decade of chaos, lawbreaking and excess.

The house's connection to that exciting time ensures that it will forever remain more than a mere structure to be possessed. It is a piece of Windsor/Essex history, a monument to an epic decade in the region's story. Steeped in legend, it shouts with historical significance. The house was imagined, made possible and constructed when precious liquor shipments were protected at the point of a gun and whisked across the waterways of the international border in high-powered boats. In its early days, Al Capone, the Chicago mobster they called Scarface, would slip across the border to do business with Harry Low and stop by to join him for a quiet drink before heading home.

When the dust settled on the 1920s, Windsor/Essex settled back with it. Those who had thrived on its excesses were determined to shut the door on their recent past. Those who had so recently shared in the overindulgence that fuelled Harry Low's success turned their backs on him.

After Harry Low died in 1955, writer Tom Butson produced a brief memoir of the man that described the transition this way:

Associates who had been eager to share the attractive, if somewhat shady deals of the '20s suddenly became church-going businessmen to whom speedboats meant fishing, and liquor was something poured from a decanter and not from a dark riverside dock. Gone were the days when machine-guns protected valuable liquor cargoes.

After Low lost the house in 1934, it passed through a succession of owners, ultimately degenerating in the early years of this millennium into a shadow of its former grandeur. Crumbling from water damage, yet bolstered by strong fundamentals to stubbornly withstand the elements, the house was purchased in 2012 by Myslichuk. He had admired and dreamed of the house for a dozen years, so when the opportunity arose, he vowed he would buy it and return it to the splendour it had exhibited in that long-gone era. He would give the house the chance to live again, to make it once more a place of laughter and fun.

The house: Construction on Devonshire Lodge began in the latter half of 1927 and was completed in the spring of 1928.

After two years of painstaking restoration, Myslichuk was sufficiently satisfied with his progress that he moved in to the home in June 2014, although his work continues. Furnishing its 4,800 square feet is an ongoing project as he studies old photographs and lets the house "speak" to him about what is right and proper. Then there is the matter of the adjacent garage and servant's quarters, a project that waits another day – and a building that Myslichuk suspects possesses an intriguing story of its own.

Ah, yes, the stories. Vern Myslichuk has certainly not overlooked the mysterious corners and cubbyholes around the property, places that beckon him to take a closer look. It is these special places from which legends are born about tunnels and secret caches, places created by Harry Low, it is said, their purpose and location lost in the murky depths of history. They are the mystery, the intrigue that imbues this house with special powers, powers that prick at your skin as you move from room to room.

This, then, is a story about one of the region's most prominent homes, a monster piece of real estate that has become a Walkerville legend. It is a story told through the life and times of the man who imagined and built it, and through the eyes of a second man who, in our own era, employed his sheer grit and determination to restore it to its full magnificence, a place that once again shouts proudly at passersby: Look at me!

Two women pass some of the Hiram Walker and Sons buildings along Walkerville's Wyandotte Street East in the early 1900s. (Courtesy Library of Congress)

Chapter 2:

Walkerville

AS HARRY LOW ROSE TO THE TOP of the heap as the most audacious rumrunner of Windsor's Prohibition era, he chose a place to build his dream home he knew would shout his success to the world. He understood there was no better spot in the Border Cities region to demonstrate that he had arrived than Walkerville. He could live no place else.

Walkerville began its existence as the company town built by the American-born whisky baron, Hiram Walker. Unlike most company towns, however, it was never designed to shut down in the event the business that had given birth to it ceased to exist. As it matured, Walkerville would evolve as a special kind of place – a garden community – patterned on the design established for similar English towns in the late 19th century.

Before anyone had ever thought of the garden community movement, though, Hiram Walker established his company town in the 1850s with the purchase of 500 acres just east of Windsor, a little town on the western frontier of the British province of Canada West. He set up a farm, a distillery and flour mill. On the farm he grew crops and raised livestock. For a time, Walker moved his family from Detroit to Walkerville, but after about five years, they moved back to the American side of the Detroit River, leaving Walker to make the daily crossing by private boat to his office on the Canadian side of the border. That private boat would eventually evolve into a public ferry service.

The village, originally known as Walker Town and later Walkerville, started off modestly. It consisted of five east/west streets that ran parallel to the river – Sandwich (now Riverside Drive), Assumption, Brant, Wyandotte and Tuscarora – and the north/south streets named First, Second, Third, Fourth and Fifth. In 1869, just two years after Confederation, Walkerville became an official Canadian post office village, but remained an unincorporated village in the township of Sandwich East.

Hiram Walker and Sons expanded its worldwide markets and spirit sales boomed. The company town grew right along with it. Staff were taken care of, housed in company built cottages, and served by shops

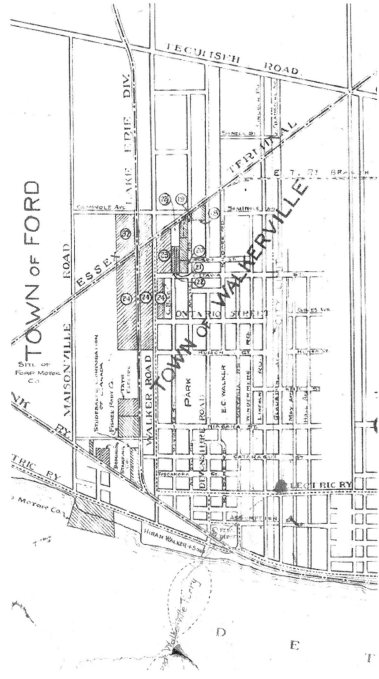

A map of the town of Walkerville in the early 1900s. (Courtesy City of Windsor Geomatics Division)

and other services provided by Hiram Walker. Walker ruled the community with an iron fist, a benevolent despot acting as its unofficial mayor.

Walkerville advanced from post office village to incorporated town in 1890 and at that time, the Detroit Journal newspaper dubbed it "the queerest, quaintest place in all Christendom." Presumably this was intended as some sort of compliment, but perhaps one tinged with a pinch of astonishment that such an undemocratic place could exist in the shadow of the United States.

With incorporation, Walkerville was about to see big changes, changes that would add a touch of democracy even as they reinforced the town's image as the finest place to live in the region.

Over time, Walker's children took on more responsibility in the family firm and introduced a more refined tone to the company town. Some of them moved to Walkerville and built houses. The numbered streets had already been renamed Kildare, Devonshire, Argyle, Monmouth and Walker roads, a touch of civility that was said to have been spurred by Hiram Walker's wife, Mary, before she died in 1872. Now there would be other more substantial changes.

Along with Walkerville's incorporation, the family established the Walkerville Land and Building Company to manage its real estate holdings. Hiram's son, Edward Chandler Walker, was named president and served in that post for many years, with other Walker family members acting as directors. Once established, the company set out to sell the remaining holdings to private individuals. Yet while the family's stranglehold over Walkerville was loosening, strict planning controls enabled it to continue to guide development.

This was about the time that the garden community movement began to take hold in England. Under the guidance of Sir Ebenezer Howard and the inspiration of the Utopian novel, Looking Backward, garden communities were being created to combine the best of town and country living.

These communities were designed to be fully self-sufficient. Besides housing, they included a district where industries would be located, as well as services, shops, community facilities and open public spaces — places where those of all income levels and walks of life could come together to enjoy the invigorating effects of outdoor life. Normally there was a greenbelt. Local food production was encouraged, and often the towns included space for entire farms.

Walkerville would be one such self-contained community. As in other garden communities, there were tree-lined avenues, sidewalks and places to encourage walking and bicycling. Even the apparently "disrupted" route of Devonshire Road, as it stops at one side of the Walker-built St. Mary's Anglican Church and starts again on the other side, was an intentional design element created in the garden community pattern.

Walkerville sat next to the larger city of Windsor and despite its size, the Walkers made sure it featured all the facilities its citizens needed to enjoy a full life of commerce and play. No one who lived there need venture in to the "dirty city." There was even a yacht club and a golf club with tennis facilities.

The Walkerville Golf Club property extended between Monmouth and Devonshire roads, running

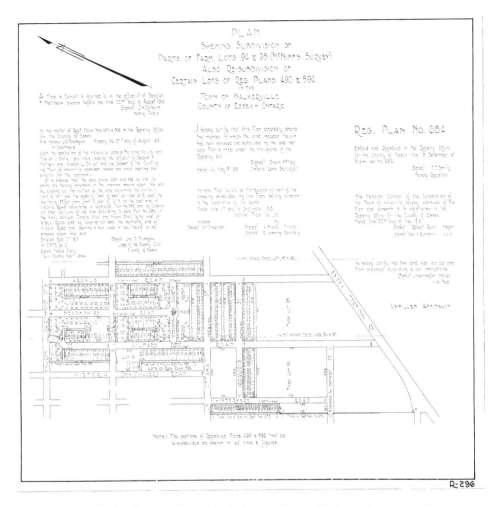

A plan of subdivision from 1913 put forth by the Walkerville Land & Building Company and Charles Chilver. (Courtesy City of Windsor Geomatics Division)

MONMOUTH ROAD

TERRACE HOUSING ON MONMOUTH ROAD (4TH STREET), BUILT BETWEEN 1893 AND 1904, REMAINS TODAY AS A REFLECTION OF THE 19TH CENTURY'S INDUSTRIAL REVOLUTION ATTITUDE TOWARD WORKERS' RESIDENTIAL NEEDS. THE WALKERVILLE LAND & BUILDING COMPANY, UNDER THE DIRECTION OF THE HIRAM WALKER & SONS DISTILLERY, COMMISSIONED DETROIT ARCHITECTS MASON & RICE AND ALBERT KAHN TO CREATE RENTAL HOUSING FOR EMPLOYEES AS PART OF THE EARLY DEVELOPMENT OF THE TOWN OF WALKERVILLE. THE TERRACES SERVED AS A BUFFER BETWEEN WALKER ROAD INDUSTRIES ON THE EAST, AND MANAGEMENT RESIDENCES TO THE WEST. BY 1933-34, ALL UNITS WERE OFFERED FOR SALE ON THE OPEN MARKET.

CITY OF WINDSOR 1992

The Walker family influence is seen today throughout Walkerville. Hiram Walker's office, top left, houses the Canadian Club Brand Centre. Terrace homes along Monmouth Road were built for company employees. Willistead Manor was built by one of Walker's sons. Walkerville Brewery is housed in a former Hiram Walker warehouse.

St. Mary's Memorial Church, Walkerville, Ontario, Canada. —11

St. Mary's Anglican Church was built by the children of Hiram and Mary Walker in 1904 to honour their parents.

Border Cities: The term referred to the municipalities of Windsor, Walkerville, Ford City (later renamed East Windsor), Riverside, Sandwich and Ojibway. It was in popular usage by 1918 when the local daily newspaper was purchased by a new owner who rechristened it the Border Cities Star. The paper became the Windsor Daily Star in 1935 with amalgamation of those communities under the name Windsor.

south from what is now Niagara Street, to Ontario Street and beyond. In later years, after club members decided the course lacked proper drainage and insisted it be moved, the land was developed into housing along what is now called Willistead Crescent, while property was set aside for the construction in 1922 of Walkerville Collegiate Institute.

Over the years, the Walkers provided fire and police protection, a waterworks system, street lighting, churches, schools and regular ferry service to Detroit. Several Walker-owned industries were established along the Walker Road strip, including a foundry, sugar refinery, basket manufacturer, brewery, brickyard, bridge manufacturing company, furniture company and lumber yard. By the time Hiram Walker died in 1899, Walker Road had become so built up with industry the area was being dubbed the Birmingham of Canada.

The town could also boast plenty of retail shops,

and on the second floor of one of them was a music hall that could accommodate up to 600 for community events. Before there was a proper commercial bank, employees of the Walker family enterprises confidently deposited their savings in the "Walker bank."

As part of the beautification process, the original employee cottages were replaced with brick terrace houses – some of which can still be seen along Monmouth Road – and semi-detached houses. Grander single-family residences were erected for the company managers, clergy and family members. The family firm brought in American architects Mason & Rice, and Albert Kahn, to design fine residences and public buildings that contributed to the ambience they sought.

As land was sold to private individuals, controls were imposed to ensure a certain grandeur and quality to the homes that were to be built. Among the controls on some blocks was a minimum size requirement of 3,500 square feet. Beautification was encouraged. Annual contests were held to choose the finest gardens, flowerbeds and most attractive homes.

As the 20th century dawned, Walkerville had evolved into an attractive and prosperous community with some of the finest residences in the region. While many of its neighbours had to settle for muddy streets, outdoor toilets and limited water supplies, Walkerville boasted paved and shady streets, modern sewers and the latest in waterworks systems.

That meant that as the strings were loosened on real estate ownership and the Walkers encouraged new blood, some of the more prosperous families from the other Border Cities were enticed to take up residence there. Many clambered to live close to the magnificent Willistead Manor, an Edwardian mansion built by Edward Chandler Walker in 1906 and surrounded by 16 acres of parkland.

Growth pressures forced the town to expand southward, and new houses were built all the way to Ottawa Street and beyond.

In 1926, the Walker family operated the second-largest distillery in Canada. That year, they sold Hiram Walker and Sons to an even larger firm, Gooderham and Worts, an expanding distillery that had been purchased three years earlier by Prince Edward County-born industrialist tycoon Harry Hatch.

Walkerville's association with the Walker family was shrinking rapidly and in 1935, the town amalgamated with Windsor (along with Sandwich and Ford City or East Windsor) to create the new City of Windsor. Despite the official demise of the town as a separate entity and the departure of the Walkers, the pattern had been well-established for the maintenance of a proud, independent-minded community within the larger municipality.

The lure of Walkerville was difficult to resist. It was a neighbourhood of fine homes and a strong historical presence. As such, it attracted many of those in search of a home in a special sort of neighbourhood.

In the decade before amalgamation, one of them was Harry Low.

Harry Low. (Financial Post)

Chapter 3:

The Arrival of Harry Low

OTTAWA'S BYWARD MARKET SITS EAST of the Rideau Canal, east of Parliament Hill, in a historic area of the city known as Lower Town. Today, ByWard Market is an area of upscale shops, bars, nightclubs and restaurants, of pricey condos and rental flats, as well as a farmers' market that has occupied space here for well over a century. This is the place where the predecessor of the modern city of Ottawa – Bytown – was established. Before its modern-day transformation, it witnessed the coming and going of countless waves of immigrants. It was a place filled with hotels and taverns, hawkers and peddlers, prostitution, lawlessness and, in the pre-Confederation era, a healthy dose of political brawls.

On March 17, 1888, it is also the place where Harry Low was born, at 127 George Street. Long before ByWard Market was transformed into a trendy district for fine dining and drinking, the first-born child of Frank and Sarah Ann (McCullough) Low entered the world in a neighbourhood where working-class people conducted business and lived in modest and sometimes even squalid apartments set overtop butcher shops, dry goods stores and sleazy entertainment palaces.

Harry, who was never known to have possessed a middle name, was the Lows' first-born child. Over the next dozen years, four more children would be born to the couple: Harry's sisters Lilian and Irene in 1891 and 1895, and brothers Samuel James and Frank Sydney in 1897 and 1900. Their father was a machinist by trade and ran his own shop in an alleyway behind Rideau Street, around the corner from where they lived. Frank Low's chosen trade made it possible for Harry to train at his side as a tool and die maker during his teenage years. After his apprenticeship, Harry worked for a time at his father's Lower Town shop.

On June 17, 1908, at the age of 20, Harry married Norah Ellen Morgan, in Ottawa, and the couple moved in to an apartment at 347 Dalhousie Street, a short walk from where his parents lived. Norah, whose name was frequently spelled without the "h" and who throughout her life was usually called Nellie, had been born in Kingston, the daughter of a military man, the same year as Harry. The couple had two

Harry Low spent his early years in Ottawa. (Courtesy Bruce Low)

children, daughter Norah Ellen in 1910 and a son, Frank Gordon, in 1916.

As an adult, Harry is described as "a big burly fellow with thick black hair and a round smiling face." He is five feet, 10 inches tall. He is known to be disarmingly gentle with a retiring nature. Friends and family also know him as an ambitious individual with a mind that is constantly coming up with plans to improve the lot of himself and his family. While working with his father at the machine shop, he saved enough money to purchase a public hall at 299 Bank Street, a place called St. George's Theatre. In the days before "talkies," silent moving pictures were featured at the St. George's and for those who couldn't afford to buy a ticket, Harry had a screen out on the street where people would gather to catch a glimpse of the action.

When the hall wasn't being used to show movies, it was rented out for public gatherings and lectures. On the side, Low would buy horses and fatten them up on bread, then sell them for a profit. Between the horses and the St. George's, Low had a nice source of added income to help him improve the family's lifestyle.

Now he was the owner of a thriving Bank Street business in what was called Upper Town, an area not far from some of the city's better residential districts. With the resulting improvement in social status, Harry Low's reputation undoubtedly rose as well. After all, the area of Bank Street where the theatre sat featured some of the city's premier shops. But the Lows still lived in "the market" and as far as Low was concerned, it didn't suit the style to which he was becoming accustomed. It wasn't long before he began looking around for a more fashionable address at which to raise his family.

The official residence of the Governor General of Canada is known as Rideau Hall, a sprawling estate that sits across Sussex Drive from the Ottawa River in an area of Ottawa known as New Edinburgh, one of the city's original settlements. On the south side of the estate farthest from the river, Rideau Hall backs onto Dufferin Road and it was on this street, in a townhouse at 72 Dufferin Road, where Harry Low moved his family in 1911. That is the address listed in the city directory as the Low family home in that year. The directory lists him as a machinist but by 1915 he is manager of St. George's Theatre, with no reference to the trades of machinist or tool and die maker.

When they looked out the front door of their Dufferin Road townhouse, Harry and Nellie Low could gaze into the treed estate of Canada's vice-regal, representative of King George V. The family had come a long way since they first married and began raising a family in that cramped apartment in the market.

On the world stage, the Great War, known today as the First World War, ground to a halt in November 1918. The social and economic changes brought about by that war would be staggering. For a start, thousands of young Canadian and American men had lost their lives in the fighting and from the many associated illnesses and diseases they contracted in the trenches and hospitals. As a result, a great number of young women across North America were coming to the realization that they were not likely to find eligible partners with whom to raise families.

If family life is not in the cards, some of them

Flappers evolved from the post-war changes in society and had a large impact on the 1920s.

began to think, they might as well enjoy life in other less conventional ways. Seeing themselves as liberated from the traditional expectations of family, a number of women decided it was quite acceptable for them to drink, smoke, dance and party. This is the beginning of the era of the Flapper, a relatively small subculture that will leave an indelible imprint on society and set the stage for a lifestyle that will help to make Harry Low a very wealthy man.

But Low isn't thinking of that quite yet. Something else has attracted his attention. Despite little formal education beyond his apprenticeship, he possesses a keen mind and notices that down at the boot toe end of the province of Ontario, in the border city of Windsor, things are beginning to happen economically. In the post-war years the automotive industry, which began across the border in Michigan, was thriving as North Americans commenced their love affair with the car.

The Ford Motor Company had first come to Windsor in 1904 and set up shop at the Walkerville Wagon Works factory, but car production remained limited until the post-war boom set in. Now with the war over, development in Windsor was taking off, and Low looked at the opportunities that presented themselves to an ambitious young entrepreneur who possessed the skills of a tool and die maker. Living in the Windsor area, he realized, would also give him easy access to opportunities in Detroit, at the time the fourth-largest metropolis in the United States and just a river's width away.

In 1919, the area on the Canadian side of the river was a conglomeration of separate municipalities – the city of Windsor and the smaller communities of Sandwich, Walkerville, Ford City and Riverside and, farther downriver, Ojibway. Together, these communities were coming to be known as the Border Cities, a term enhanced in 1918 when W.F. Herman purchased the Windsor Record and renamed it the Border Cities Star.

In 1919, Harry and Nellie Low sold the St. George's Theatre, packed up their household, and moved to Sandwich, the small town on Windsor's western flank. Over the next few years, they would live at a number of addresses on Caron Avenue and Askin Boulevard. For a smart young businessman setting up in this fast-paced region, the prospects looked bright. And while it seems unlikely Low thought about it at the time, the United States Congress was about to make those prospects a whole lot brighter. Prohibition was about to be ushered in to existence.

Shutting down the gin joints

In Canada as well as in the United States, the ideas that led to Prohibition began to take hold in the 19th century. That had been an era of cheap and easy access to alcohol, to often squalid working conditions, a lack of understanding of the long-term impact of liquor, family violence and the rise of the women's rights movement. Cheap liquor encouraged overworked male factory labourers to take refuge in the temporary comfort it offered. This in turn sparked violence against women and children in the home, creating a cause ready made for religious leaders intent on stamping out the "demon rum" and suffragettes fighting for women's rights.

Ontario had given municipalities the right to vote "dry" as far back as 1876, and by the outbreak of the First World War in 1914, quite a number of them had done just that. Then in the midst of the war, in 1916, the Ontario legislature enacted a Temperance Act that created a blanket prohibition across the province on the sale of beer and liquor - but not wine - while making exceptions for its medicinal use. This loophole led to thousands of doctors' "prescriptions" being written, with lineups for prescriptions growing particularly long just prior to the Christmas season!

Humorist Stephen Leacock brought his own gently wicked wit to the issue of liquor-by-prescription when he wrote: "To get a drink during Prohibition it is necessary to go to the drugstore and lean up against the counter making a gurgling sigh like apoplexy. One often sees these apoplexy cases lined up four deep."

When Ontario held a referendum to gauge the popularity of its Prohibition policy in 1919, Windsor, never a city to run with the crowd, was one of only three municipalities to oppose it. While the act remained in force until 1927 when the Liquor Control Board was established, Prohibition proved to be no more successfully imposed in Ontario than it was in the United States, where it dragged on until 1933.

Prohibition unfolded quite differently in Canada than it did in the U.S., however. Prohibitionists in this country quickly came up against that unique Canadian conundrum of shared federal and provincial responsibilities. That fact meant the provinces were responsible for sale and consumption, while Parliament held sway over the manufacture and trade in alcoholic beverages.

In March 1918, the federal government prohibited, for the rest of the war (until November that same year), the manufacture and importation of alcohol into provinces that had outlawed it already. This applied to Ontario, which had shuttered drinking establishments and forbade the sale of alcoholic beverages, as well as its possession and consumption outside of private dwellings.

However, there were exceptions. Alcohol could still be purchased for industrial, scientific, mechanical, artistic, sacramental (wine) and medicinal purposes. As well, distillers and brewers could still make their products and sell them outside their province.

Once the war was over and full-scale production was allowed again, eager entrepreneurs ensured liquor was readily available for sale through illegal drinking establishments across the province – places known as blind pigs and speakeasies.

Legally speaking, things were much more cut-and-dried in the United States. Congress passed full Prohibition in 1919 and with the states' ratification, it came into force in 1920. This created a huge and thirsty market for whatever beer and liquor Canada could manage to produce and export. With Canada now the great supplier of alcoholic beverages to the United States, all that was needed was a reliable crew of suppliers.

Enter, Harry Low.

The barons of booze

Cocaine Cowboys is a 2006 documentary that follows the arrival of cocaine into Miami in the 1970s and '80s, and the impact that trade had on crime, law enforcement and society. There were the logistics of importation and elaborate distribution networks to be established, as well as the expense of setting up the infrastructure required to carry out this highly lucrative business. The film claims that much of the economic growth that took place in Miami is a direct offshoot of that illegal trade. It also gave birth to the 1980s television phenomenon known as Miami Vice.

In a very real sense, Miami's experience repeated what had happened in Windsor in the 1920s. Back then, the "cocaine cowboys" were the rumrunners, the barons of booze.

Harry Low arrived in the Border Cities at just the

right time. Low was always on the lookout for ways to supplement his income as a tool and die maker. In Ottawa, he had done well from his movie theatre and public hall. In the Border Cities, he believed his ticket to a wealthier life would be a pool hall, and soon after moving to the area he opened one up at 100 Sandwich Street West.

Today, a large portion of what used to be called Sandwich Street is now named Riverside Drive. Low's Sandwich Street pool hall was located near the northwest corner of what is now Riverside and Ferry Street, on the rise overlooking downtown Detroit.

Harry Low's establishment was known by a number of names: the Border Cities Billiard Parlour, Harry's Recreation Room and Harry's Pool Room. It didn't take long for it to be known by its most important name: A great place to buy a drink.

But first, he had to find the money to buy alcohol to resell to his eager customers. He borrowed $300, tracked down a supplier – not difficult at all in the Windsor of 1919 – and created his own blind pig and gambling joint in the back room of the pool hall. It became an instant success, popular not just with Windsorites, but with American whisky tourists who were beginning to flock to the Canadian side of the river in search of their alcoholic beverages.

In these, the early days of U.S. Prohibition, thousands of ordinary Canadian citizens discovered that it could be very lucrative to buy a few bottles of alcohol, take the ferry to Detroit and sell them either on the street or to shop owners. A good bottle of Canadian whisky could be picked up from a supplier for $2.50 in Windsor and sold just a mile across the river for $10. What could be easier?

Overnight, an entire kitchen industry of smuggling small quantities of alcohol grew up along the Canada-U.S. border. While saloons throughout the Border Cities were shut up tight, the export of Canadian alcoholic beverages quickly created a long line of export docks along the riverfront, from Amherstburg to Riverside. Dock workers were kept hopping to fill the cargo holds of the growing number of motor launches and rowboats that were pulling up, night and day, to stock up with the booze that was being demanded and easily sold across the border.

Looking back at the era today, it is easy to forget that throughout the 1920s, the business itself of exporting alcoholic beverages was perfectly legal in Canada. Under Canadian federal law, it was legal to produce beer and liquor and to export these products to destinations outside of Ontario, provided they paid their taxes. In effect, Ottawa could not care less where the liquor was going, as long as it collected its tax revenue. While United States authorities were irritated by this fact and lobbed a regular series of threats across the border, there was little they could do to stop it.

What was illegal in Ontario, however, was the practice of leaving a Windsor export dock with a load of booze and then turning around to deliver that cargo to a spot on the Ontario coastline, a process known as short-circuiting. This happened frequently and became the supply line for the speakeasies – such as the one at Harry's Pool Room – that kept Ontarians well lubricated until the province established the LCBO and allowed beer makers to create the Brewers' Retail corporation in 1927.

Ontario did relax its full ban in 1924 by allowing

CPR station: The Canadian Pacific Railway station on Sandwich Street West in Windsor was built in 1887 and used by the railway until 1917. Harry Low leased it for use as his Carling Export office, a place where he held legendary parties. It was demolished in 1935.

the sale of a low-alcohol beer, though this "near-beer" was widely scorned and the illegal full-strength brew remained the preferred libation.

But the pool hall was becoming less of a priority for Low. It didn't take him long to comprehend the opportunities that existed in "going big." Low became the accredited agent in Windsor for a number of Montreal brewers' and distillers' export wings.

So by the early 1920s, Harry Low was a successful purveyor and exporter of alcoholic beverages. He'd started to create a good life for his wife and children and moved to ever-nicer homes that he felt better reflected his rising status. But wouldn't it be nice to be able to live in Walkerville? he thought. Then there would be no question: everyone would know of Harry Low's success.

In 1923, Low took his biggest step yet in the business world when he partnered with Marco Leon of Windsor and Londoner Charles Burns to buy out the old Carling Brewing Company. Carling had been founded in the early 1800s, but with Prohibition turning the industry on its head, it had faltered, its management unable to cope with the new business realities. The trio leased the former Canadian Pacific Railway station on Sandwich Street West at the foot of Caron Avenue, and turned it into the headquarters for Carling and a new export combine, the Bermuda Export Company.

The combine had been Low's idea as a method of co-ordinating distillers and brewers to prevent them from undercutting one another's prices. It seemed a natural turn of events that Low would act as Bermuda Export's chief of operations.

Harry Low had arrived. As he grew wealthier,

Harry Low leased the elegant former CPR station for the offices of Erie Transit and his other associated companies.

he planned for the day that he could build his own home, a spacious mansion that would reflect his new-found wealth.

On February 7, 1923, Harry and Nellie Low took a break from business and went on a trip to Europe. They sailed cross the Atlantic first-class, visiting England and France on a five-week tour. Maybe it was during this trip, observing the sights and the architecture of the Old World, that made the couple visualize what their own home might look like some day. Maybe they saw the Cotswold cottage roofs in England and the grand stone manor houses that dotted the countryside. The Lows' grandson, Bruce Low, believes one of the buildings that made an impression on them was a big old stone railway station they came upon.

When they returned to Canada, the Lows came back to their home at 220 Askin Boulevard in Sandwich and that summer, purchased their first home in Walkerville, at 262 Devonshire Road (its modern-day address is 1144 Devonshire). Undoubtedly, their heads were now filled with visions of the grand buildings they had seen on their trip. Perhaps they saw their new home as a stopover on their way to their true desire, to build their own custom-designed Walkerville mansion.

Booze and the mobs

No single factor contributed more to the rise of organized crime on this continent than U.S. Prohibition. While the export of alcoholic beverages had at first been conducted mostly on a small scale, by housewives, daily cross-border commuters and men paddling across the Detroit River in their canoes, organized crime awoke to the realization in the early '20s of the immense profits that were there for the taking. In Chicago, Al Capone ruled the liquor trade. In Detroit, Capone remained respectful and wary of a vicious mob that became known as the Purple Gang.

The Purple Gang moved forcefully to sew up the lucrative business of importing Canadian alcohol into Detroit. By 1924, Low had established himself as a well-known purveyor of spirits in the Border Cities area. It became apparent to the Purple Gang that if they were going to partner with a Canadian agent, that agent ought to be Harry Low.

It shouldn't come as much of a surprise, then, that emissaries from the Purple Gang would come calling at the door of Harry Low. This they did, one early July day in 1924. Low was instructed to attend a "meeting" on a dark back road out in the country, in what is today the town of Tecumseh. Intrigued by the offer, Low complied, and that night, he drove his Model T to the secret rendezvous.

The men he met there told him that if he accepted their offer to supply them with Canadian beer and liquor, he would become richer than he could ever imagine. Low could become their chief Canadian supplier, he was told. As long as the booze kept flowing, so would the money. As a sign of good faith, Low was handed a suitcase and told not to open it until he got home. There was a thinly veiled threat attached, too. If he didn't comply with their "invitation," these emissaries would come calling for their suitcase.

When Low arrived home, he placed the suitcase on the kitchen table and opened it. Inside was $80,000 cash.

"Nellie," he called to his wife. "Come here. I've got something to show you. Now we're really in the whisky business."

The triumvirate of booze

Low never believed in doing anything small if he could do it big. He had started off with alcohol and gambling in the back of his pool hall, then progressed to the export trade and then to the brewery business and eventually he would expand into distilleries too. The two-bit, mom-and-pop rumrunners were being wrung from the business, muscled out by U.S.-based organized crime. It was these people with whom Harry Low would be doing business, not only as the agent who took possession and arranged sale of the product, but as a brewer and distiller as well.

As commerce began to flourish, Low had been followed to the city by his brothers, Sam and Syd, and their parents, Frank and Sarah Ann. Syd was the only one of the three brothers to have never joined in the business of booze. By 1922, Sam was working for Harry at the billiards hall and a year later, as Harry's liquor dealings began to take ever more of his time, Sam was appointed manager of the hall. Later, after Carling Brewing was transformed into the Carling Export Brewing and Malting Company, Sam was appointed manager and their father, Frank, was named proprietor of the pool hall.

Burns, Leon and Low were the triumvirate of booze at Carling Export. Burns was made president, the gentlemanly face of the corporation. Leon was the man on the street, handling problems as they arose and making sure no one stood in the way of progress and profits. Harry Low was vice-president and ran the all-important Windsor docks export operation under the Bermuda Export moniker. There was no doubt which man was really in charge, though. When a Canadian government Royal Commission was established to look into whether the nation's brewers and distillers were paying all of the tax they owed, it termed the Bermuda Export combine "Low's group."

Harry Low was accumulating a great deal of wealth and power from his growing empire. They say there was a bit of a strut in Low's walk, a swagger about him. He was a big man with a square, somewhat heavy-looking face. He combed his thick wavy hair up into a pompadour. That, plus the bow tie he always wore, lent him a sporty appearance that gained for him the nickname Dapper Dan.

Harry Low and partners bought Carling Brewing Company in 1923. (Courtesy Bruce Low)

The Vedas was one of two ships Harry Low purchased to expand his alcohol exporting venture. (Windsor Star)

Big business

The export of liquor and beer was a huge business in Canada during the 1920s and a significant source of revenue for the federal government. It became evident, though, that a large portion of these beverages was getting through tax-free. As an example, in 1926 the federal government recorded $26 million in total exports, but when a federal inquiry looked more closely, it estimated that $40 million worth had crossed from the Windsor and area docks alone that year. The border was proving to be a very leaky one.

It has been estimated that of all the alcohol that flowed across the Canada/U.S. border during Prohibition, three-quarters of it went through the Windsor/Essex frontier. By the mid-1920s, most of the small Canadian entrepreneur/smugglers had been eliminated, replaced by organized crime from the U.S. With the creation of the Bermuda Export combine and the new arrangements with the Purple Gang that controlled the bulk of imports into Detroit and area, Harry Low and his partners held sway over a significant portion of that export trade.

But Low felt he could do better. To further extend his reach, he purchased two decommissioned British minesweepers, the Vedas (originally named HMCS Shearwater) and the Geronimo. After its career as a minesweeper, the Vedas had also spent some time as a sealer and even a banana boat. Low had grander plans. Montreal was a huge producer of liquor and beer, and yet the primary crossing point to the United States was 1,000 kilometres to the southwest. He would use the ships to carry the beverages to where they were needed.

The ships would come to the western basin of Lake Erie, or else the Detroit River or Lake St. Clair. There they would lie at anchor overnight. During the hours of dark, smaller, swifter vessels would approach from the American shore, offload the cargo from Low's big ships and head back to the U.S. Sometimes, one or the other of the ships would head to the Atlantic and pick up liquor from Halifax, then sail down the coastline and sit outside the U.S. territorial limits, where the same procedure would be applied.

U.S. agents were constantly on the lookout for these transactions and stepped up their vigilance as the 1920s progressed. Once, the Geronimo was seized by the Americans and towed to a dock in Wayne, Michigan. Later they blamed a "storm" for loosening the ship's moorings. The same storm, no doubt, that directed the ship back across the river and safely into the hands of Harry Low.

Audacity in action

Low's audacity became legendary. He was a constant thorn in the side of the Ontario government, which tried its best to stem the flow of illegal liquor and beer. And when the province decided to fight the rumrunners by ending its own Prohibition and setting up a sales system in 1927, Low didn't hesitate to fight back.

Ontario's liquor czar, LCBO chief Sir Henry Drayton, fired a volley at Low and his colleagues when he obtained a court order to seize $1 million worth of liquor sitting on Windsor's export docks on July 11, 1928. The move came in the wake of a decision that stopped the full-scale storage of alcoholic beverages waiting for export. It was an early version of just-in-time delivery: The exporters' only option,

Harry Low's ship, the Vedas, sits in the Detroit River as a tug comes alongside. In the background is downtown Detroit while on the left, a ferry chugs toward Windsor. (Courtesy Bruce Low)

said the province, was to deliver their product directly to the waiting boats by truck and rail.

This would not do. There were two reasons the export docks were so valuable to Low and the other exporters and why they needed to stockpile massive supplies in warehouses along the Windsor waterfront. First, it allowed them to take advantage when the best opportunities arose to move their product across the border – that is, when the American authorities weren't looking. Drayton's just-in-time order would allow American authorities to pick off the smuggling booze-runners at will.

The second reason for the export docks was to make it easier to "short-circuit" supplies to the U.S. and bring them back to the Canadian shore for distribution to blind pigs on this side of the border. And make no mistake, as the baron of booze, Harry Low was well aware that Canadian-made liquor and beer was being resold, illegally, in Ontario. As the owner of Harry's Pool Hall, he was buying it himself. When Ontario returned to the legal sale of alcoholic beverages in 1927, it was threatening the livelihood of big exporters such as Harry Low.

To enforce his order, LCBO chief Drayton sent the OPP swooping in to seize and hold the supplies and then dared the rumrunners to make the next move. In the meantime, a well-armed contingent stood vigil over the supplies.

"The police are taking no chances whatever of a possible attack by hijackers from the river," reported the Border Cities Star, "and are receiving the full co-operation of the Windsor police … (I)t is not inconceivable that Detroit rum-running gangs might make a bold and desperate attempt to reopen the channels by attacking the Carling (Low's) and Nathanson docks. All through the night the provincial policemen were closely on watch."

The attack would not come from the U.S., or the river, however. Within days, as provincial authorities awaited a legal move on the part of the rumrunners, a daring daylight stunt left authorities, and police, standing in stupefied silence.

It started when an apparent runaway Model T Ford roared down the hill of a Windsor street, bounced off a dock and sailed high into the air before it came splashing down into the Detroit River. A crowd gathered and police rushed to the scene. After some effort, the car was winched back to shore and it was assumed the passengers had been swept downriver, likely to their deaths. Police dragged the river for bodies all afternoon as curious onlookers lined the riverbank.

An anonymous telephone tip to police the next day revealed what had happened. As police searched in vain for the bodies of victims of the horrible mishap, three large trucks, loaded with alcoholic beverages, left the Carling export docks and headed along the river road to a quieter location. Within minutes, hundreds of cases of fine Canadian whisky were on their way across the river on a fleet of speedboats and minutes after that, had been loaded into trucks for distribution to waiting American imbibers.

Harry Low had struck. Flamboyant, audacious, devil-may-care Harry Low.

Harry Low reached the pinnacle of his success by 1928, but trouble loomed. (Courtesy Bruce Low)

Tricks of the trade

The Royal Commission on Customs and Excise, established to track unpaid liquor taxes, began its cross-country hearings in 1927. Delving in to Low's affairs, it discovered a purposefully complicated tangle of associations and business dealings aimed at making it as difficult as possible to follow the trail of money.

As an example, an entity called the Erie Transit Company handled both Carling and Seagram beverages, while Seagram also used its own Seagram's Distilling Agency – an organization on which Low's brother, Sam, sat as vice-president. Sam Low was also listed as manager of the Carling Export Brewing and Malting Company and an executive in a number of export companies, including the Mexican Export Company, the Vancouver Forwarding Company and the Atlas Shipping Company. He was not, however, part of the Low, Burns and Leon export firm.

As they followed the complicated trail, commission auditors established that for a six-month stretch between late 1926 and early 1927, a number of Low's companies earned total profits of $500,000, for which no income tax returns were ever filed.

Another one of Low's companies, the Franco-Canadian Import Company, operated a bonded liquor warehouse in Halifax. Low, Leon and Burns were listed as directors. Testimony before the commission found "irregularities on labelling" and a stash of U.S. revenue strips used to seal bottles of liquor. One news report of the testimony concluded: "Books of liquor import company were mutilated."

The commission also discovered 6,000 cases of

beer sold by Carling to Bermuda Export that were not accounted for in Bermuda's own paperwork, leaving lawyers with the "strong impression" that the beer was actually being illegally short-circuited back in to Canada for sale. Rail shipments of beer labelled as sugar and fresh fish were also discovered by the diligent commission investigators.

The cost of doing business

The Royal Commission discovered plenty of evidence of forged documents and bribes being offered and paid to federal customs officials. One customs agent testified that after he refused to accept a bribe to allow empty beer kegs back in to Canada from the U.S. without being charged duty, he was mysteriously transferred from his post at the Bermuda Export docks.

In another example, the yardmaster at Windsor's Michigan Central Railway depot told the commission he was advised to look the other way when empty boxcars arrived listed as "loaded." The man was told to allow the empty cars to be moved to the CPR yard where they would be loaded with beer and sent back to Michigan Central, properly fitted with all the necessary Customs seals for export to the U.S. The yardmaster was told he would be handsomely rewarded.

Questioned about the incident, Low at first blamed the matter on his "half-inebriated" brother, Sam. "If it was so easy," Low joked to his questioners, "I would have availed myself of the opportunity long ago." Under further questioning and a load of evidence that the incident did actually occur, Low maintained his composure. "I was just curious to see if there was a legal way of doing it," he explained.

Looking the other way was a common practice among local authorities as well. Windsor author Patrick Brode, in his book, Unholy City, writes that it was widely known by 1927 that bootleggers were buying off the city police. In other words, police were being paid to look the other way when activities that contravened provincial liquor laws were observed. Brode writes:

During Prohibition, the police in the Border Cities had an ambivalent attitude toward alcohol. In the early 1920s, the liquor trade had become an important new industry in the Detroit River area and the border police seemed to have little inclination to interfere with it. In any case, it was left to a separate branch of the provincial police to enforce the temperance laws. For their part, the Windsor police seemed to have little use for abstinence and at the annual meeting of the Canadian Association of Chiefs of Police held in Windsor in 1927, Windsor's Chief, David Thompson, saw that glasses were full and that alcohol was served in the stationhouse.

Bruce Low lives today in Windsor and recalls how, as a boy, he and his mother were taken in by a kindly Harry and Nellie Low when his parents' marriage broke up. Harry and Nellie adopted their young grandson, and conferred the Low family name on him. Bruce Low says that while his grandmother rarely spoke of those old days, on occasion she would let her guard down and a piece of history would come forth.

MONTREAL'S SUPREME BUSINESS LOCATION

Architects:—Ross & MacDonald.
Contractors:—Geo. A. Fuller Co., Ltd.

Harry Low and his partners announce a huge office complex project in Montreal, the Dominion Square building. (Financial Post)

Indicative of their high-flying ways is this cheque for $1.5 million the three partners wrote to the corporation they created for the project. (Courtesy Bruce Low)

Nellie Low held the Windsor police in utter disdain, says her grandson. "She told me how my grandfather bought off the police in the city. She called them all crooks. Not just the police, but she said immigration looked the other way too. She had no use for law enforcement because of that. They were easily bought and yet they'd do a turnabout and try to arrest you."

As a result, Low was kept busy replenishing the supply of payments to police so he could stay in business.

Bruce Low says his grandmother recounted how police frequently came to the house to "do business" with Harry. "She said they kept some of the booze in 'some tunnels' there for times like that."

When the Royal Commission on Customs and Excise completed its investigation and reported its findings in February 1928, it noted a mountain of evidence of bribery, forgery, smuggling and bootlegging by manufacturers and export agents alike. The recommendation was that all taxes must be paid.

Harry Low was clearly the kingpin of the liquor and beer export business along the Canada-U.S. border, a fact recognized in a Maclean's Magazine article of December 1, 1928. The article, a report about the violence that had seized the region that year and titled "Men who kill for whisky", noted Low's "present position of eminence in the liquor export traffic."

Diversification

Despite the increasing troubles that faced Low and the other exporters, business was still booming and Low decided there was no better time to expand his horizons. Diversification would serve him well if the alcohol business dried up, he felt. In the summer of 1928, with Low at the peak of his success, he and his partners, Marco Leon and Charles Burns, announced plans to build what would be Canada's largest office structure, a $10 million, 10-storey edifice in downtown Montreal. Named the Dominion Square Building, it was to be erected by the partners' specially created Dominion Square Company.

"Completion of the big building will mark another step in the already wide activities of the three principals," boasted a story in the Border Cities Star. It noted that the owners of Carling Breweries already held additional property in Windsor and area valued at $2.6 million, as well as $2.3 million in Toronto property. "Mr. Low also is heavily interested in (Windsor's) Security Building and is associated with his colleagues in the erection of that structure, the border's largest office building," it said, adding that there were plans in place for yet another Windsor office structure of similar size.

The Toronto real estate was in the form of several downtown plots picked up in anticipation of the T. Eaton store looking for a place to move and expand.

Harry and Nellie Low were also planning some real estate transactions of a more personal nature. They'd lived in Walkerville since the summer of 1923 and always dreamed of building their own home there. Harry wanted a place that reflected his own brash personality and wealth, a place he could have custom designed and built.

He didn't have to look far for inspiration. Directly across the street from their beautiful yellow brick home stood the gateway to the most incredible house Windsor had ever seen. Built by rumrunner multimillionaire James Scott Cooper some years before for a reported $400,000, the 40-room mansion boasted an indoor pool, conservatory, organ that piped music throughout the house and magnificent pillared portico. The immaculate gardens featured ornate statuary and mature tree plantings.

Harry Low must have stared at that gateway regularly for four years. He must have dreamed how he, too, could make his indelible mark on Walkerville.

On July 25, 1927, Harry and Nellie Low handed over $18,750 and signed the papers to purchase a large plot of land (205 feet by 130 feet) from the Walkerville Land and Building Company, a property that looked diagonally across the street at Cooper Court and was still listed as part of the old Walkerville Country Club estate.

Here, Low would make his most enduring mark. Here, he would build a home that could never be duplicated, never surpassed. Here, he would build Devonshire Lodge.

Dominion Square Building: Built in Montreal between 1928 and 1930 in the Beaux Arts style, it featured 12 above-ground floors (the original plan called for 10) and a shopping concourse. The building houses the Montreal Gazette newspaper and the square on which it sits is now known as Dorchester Square.

Beautiful New Residence of Harry Low

THE new residence of Harry Low, at the corner of Devonshire Road and Ontario street, which will be one of the finest in the Border Cities when completed. The building will be finished outside entirely in stone, with a full thatched roof, the latter believed to be the only roof finish of its kind, on a private home, in Western Ontario. It is arranged with special shingles manufactured in British Columbia. Accompanying the house is a detached garage, with multiple car capacity, and containing also a private gymnasium. This residence is one of several "Lawton-Bilt" homes, designed and constructed under the direction of George Lawton, 7 Chatham street west, during this summer. Mr. Lawton specializes in residences of the better class, and this home is cited as an outstanding example of his work. It is anticipated that Mr. Low's home will be ready for occupancy late in the spring of next year.

A photo in the Border Cities Star November 10, 1927, shows the house under construction. (Windsor Star)

Chapter 4:

The Building of the Monster

ONCE THEY HAD THEIR CHOSEN PLOT of land, Harry Low and his wife, Nellie, went to work planning their magnificent Walkerville mansion. When it came time for Low to choose someone to turn their ideas into reality, he gave the task to a local man by the name of George Lawton. Why didn't Low select someone with grander credentials, someone who had established himself on a broader stage? The Detroit-based Albert Kahn and Mason & Rice architectural firms had designed many of the finest homes and commercial buildings in Walkerville. Why not one of them?

Maybe they were too "establishment" for the recently arrived Low. Maybe they were too staid, too unwilling to accommodate some of the wackier design ideas the eccentric rumrunner brought to the project.

Low was familiar with, and a fan of Lawton and his work by the time he decided he was ready to build his own Walkerville mansion. George Lawton's daughter, Margaret Lawton Spencer, told former Windsor city heritage planner Evelyn McLean in 1994 she believed Low had lived in a number of other homes constructed by her father. He definitely lived in at least one: the yellow brick house at 1144 Devonshire to which the Lows moved in 1923.

Low found a sympathetic ear in Lawton when the two of them sat down in 1927 to plan the monster house the rumrunner would name Devonshire Lodge. Perhaps Lawton himself felt that by taking on this project with a man who represented the rollicking side of society of 1920s Windsor, he was taking a big step toward leaving his mark as one of the area's premier builders of the modern era.

Perhaps it was Low's opportunity to "stick it to" the more pretentious Kahn and Mason & Rice agencies. Or perhaps he was showing Walkerville society a new day had dawned.

Those more established architectural firms were linked to another era in Walkerville's history. Their structures came from the late Victorian and Edwardian times, a more genteel period in the town's and the region's history. Now, with the arrival of Prohibition, the Roaring Twenties and the Flappers, a time when the entire Border Cities region had been caught up in a culture of drinking, partying and skirting the law, it was time for someone different to take over, someone more in tune with these modern times.

In his book, Unholy City, Patrick Brode writes: "By 1927, Windsor was described as the Monte Carlo of Canada."

The Monte Carlo of Canada. That wasn't a description that would go down well with the cream of Walkerville society, and yet Walkerville itself had been born out of Hiram Walker's whisky empire.

Life in the 1920s was quite far removed from that dominated by the button-down Victorians and Edwardians of the pre-war period. Clothing was different; mores were different; social activities were different. This was the Jazz Age. On the silver screen, Rudolph Valentino and Joan Crawford danced the Tango and the Charleston. As the young people danced, their parents' and grandparents' generation were scandalized by all of the touching and the hugging and the gyrations.

Much of that dancing was going on downriver from the Border Cities, on BobLo Island, where Henry Ford had hired Albert Kahn to design and build a huge dance hall that attracted fun-seeking patrons from Michigan and Ontario. While the hall had seen a more sedate clientele when it opened in 1913, by the time of the Roaring Twenties it, too, had been taken over by the new, freer era, the era when Al Jolson, Louis Armstrong and Fats Waller produced the music, when Hemmingway and F. Scott Fitzgerald wrote the literature and when Fritz Lang's futuristic city in Metropolis forced filmgoers to ponder life in a bold new way.

Harry Low was a modern man, a bold entrepreneur, a product of the 1920s. No wonder he looked for someone new, someone more daring to create his masterpiece.

Who was George Lawton?

George Ernest Lawton was a humble and self-made man, by all accounts friendly and outgoing. The same age as Harry Low, he was born November 9, 1888 near Ridgetown in nearby Kent County. He stood five-foot-11 and was described as something of a beanpole of a man. Lawton began his working life selling electrical power to farmers before going to work for London Life Insurance. In 1916, he moved to Windsor and partnered with a man named McDonald. The two of them set up an office on Pitt Street from which they sold insurance and real estate, represented mortgage companies, appraised properties and inspected buildings. It was a wide-ranging partnership that seemed destined, by the 1920s, to have landed the pair in the house-building business as well.

Lawton advertised his company as the "builder of better made homes," with insurance and real estate as other branches of the enterprise. The building wing was known as Lawton-Bilt Homes. In the mid-1920s, McDonald and Lawton collaborated on the construction of a block of houses on the south side of Ontario Street, between Devonshire and Kildare roads, across the street from the magnificent Cooper Court, and just around the corner from Harry Low's first Walkerville house.

Lawton later built other homes in Walkerville and in 1929-30 lived in one of them, at what is today 709 Devonshire. He sold the house to businessman and community activist George M. Duck in 1931, and today the home is known as the Duck House.

Popular drinking terms from the 1920s:
Gin mill: a bar
Hooch: bootleg liquor
Dead soldier: empty beer bottle

Houses on Ontario St., Walkerville, Between Devonshire and Kildare Planned and Constructed by McDonald & Lawton.

At top, George Lawton, left, and his partner at the site of Lawton-Bilt Homes construction on Ontario Street in 1926. (Courtesy Walter Donaldson)

At bottom, the same Ontario Street view today.

While blueprints for Devonshire Lodge are missing, those for another Lawton-Bilt home, this one at 2077 Willistead Crescent, list John H. Drury as designer, but no architect. (Courtesy Norman and Beverly Marshall)

Willistead Crescent: Before Willistead Crescent existed, two streets – Navaho and Cayuga – ran between Devonshire and Monmouth roads. The right-of-way for a third street, Delaware, exists on town plans but was never created, and is now covered by Walkerville Collegiate Institute.

Lawton wasn't known for employing architects for his projects. On the blueprints for a house he built on a street that is today known as Willistead Crescent, there is no architect listed and John H. Drury is simply named as "designer." No such blueprints are known to exist today for Harry Low's house so it cannot be known whether Drury or some other designer was used on the project. But Lawton's daughter believed that while he may have employed a draftsman, Lawton drew up the design himself, in co-operation with Harry Low.

Jim Cooper, whose father, Cyril, once owned Walkerville Lumber, recalls George Lawton as a skilled designer. Cooper remembers his parents taking trips to Grosse Pointe and other upscale Detroit suburbs, searching for houses that pleased their eye.

When they saw something they liked, they would photograph it. The idea was to come back and sit down with George Lawton, show him the pictures and point out details.

"That's how they came up with the idea for the home they had George build them on Ypres Street," says Cooper. "They'd see something they liked and told George and he designed and laid out the house." Lawton built the Cooper home in 1939.

Is that what Harry Low did more than a decade earlier? And if so, where did he come up with the unusual and almost bumptious ideas that went in to the creation of his life's dream? What inspired Devonshire Lodge?

Low and his wife, Nellie, had taken a voyage to England and France in 1923. In February 1927, they left on a return trip, this time for two months and this time with their two children, Norah and Frank. Was one of the reasons for their second trip to check out some of the fine architectural details that had caught their eye five years earlier? Was it the Cotswold cottages of southwest England that inspired Low to order the undulating faux thatch roof his own new home would eventually feature? It's likely, but Margaret Lawton Spencer believed Low's fascination with a home on Pine Lake Road in West Bloomfield, Michigan, played a part in the design of that roof as well.

And what about the name itself? Why did Low call his home Devonshire Lodge? To some, the term "lodge" could suggest a rustic country place, a hunting lodge or a small house at the gate of a grand estate. This would be Harry Low's lodge, his escape from the worries of his high-pressure, high-risk business.

The house sits at the corner of Ontario and

Some Lawton-Bilt Homes in Walkerville:

709 Devonshire Road. After building this house, George Lawton lived in it for about two years.

1144 Devonshire Road. Harry and Nellie Low lived here for five years before moving to Devonshire Lodge a half-block away.

1218 Devonshire Road.

2077 Willistead Crescent.

Devonshire, as much facing one as the other. Devonshire, however, is far more English-sounding than Ontario. As the name of a county or a shire in southwest England, Devonshire might have appealed to Low's newly developed affinity for the trappings of English life.

There might have also been a hint of irony in his selection of the term Devonshire Lodge, a cheeky thumbing of his nose at some of the other grand estates in the neighbourhood. There seems to be nothing the least bit modest, nothing particularly lodge-like about Devonshire Lodge. Maybe Low was telling his neighbours he was so wealthy that he could afford to poke fun at them.

'A very bizarre home'

As it rose from its foundations, Harry Low's house created a sensation in staid Old Walkerville. In November 1927, the Border Cities Star ran a photograph of its construction beneath the label, "Beautiful new residence of Harry Low." It will be "one of the finest" homes in the region, said the newspaper. The faux thatch roof was believed to be the only one of its kind in Western Ontario and was built of special shingles brought in from British Columbia.

Of Lawton-Bilt Homes the newspaper said: "Mr. Lawton specializes in residences of the better class, and this home is cited as an outstanding example of his work."

Present-day Windsor architect Jason Grossi has been familiar with Harry Low's house for a number of years, having advised its previous owner, Frank Vella, and drawn up a plan of its layout.

"Architecturally, it's a very bizarre home," he says.

"It doesn't fit into any of the vernacular architecture that was occurring at that time here in Windsor."

Grossi says he can imagine the Lows going on vacation and coming home with a suitcase full of ideas they then decided they wanted incorporated into their new home. "It doesn't look like anybody of architectural merit designed the house. It looks as though somebody saw something they liked, was rich, and wanted to implement it," Grossi says.

Windsor city heritage planner John Calhoun says, "Low is a working-class man who has found a way to make a great deal of money, and (his house) was a bit in the order of gaudy nouveau riche-showoff. Something that's unusual, that's come from some kind of an inspiration rather than following convention.

"What rich people normally did with their houses is have this squared-off look, fancy decorations and so forth. (Low) decided to go out, using an established local builder to do it, and do this most peculiar design that maybe came from some picture, or some trip to England."

Adds Grossi: "You have to ask yourself, 'who is this Harry Low character and why did he create this huge cottage with the faux thatched roof, which is not indicative of any other house in Windsor, which is angled at 45 degrees to every other house, sits at the corner in a very prominent way, and which is actually not at all like a Cotswold?'"

The house's current owner, Vern Myslichuk, who bought it in 2012, says: "I ask myself, 'how did this house get here?' It wasn't just some guy who built a house. He was making a statement. He wasn't just saying 'I'm in the rumrunning business', but 'I'm in the freaking *RUMRUNNING* business!'"

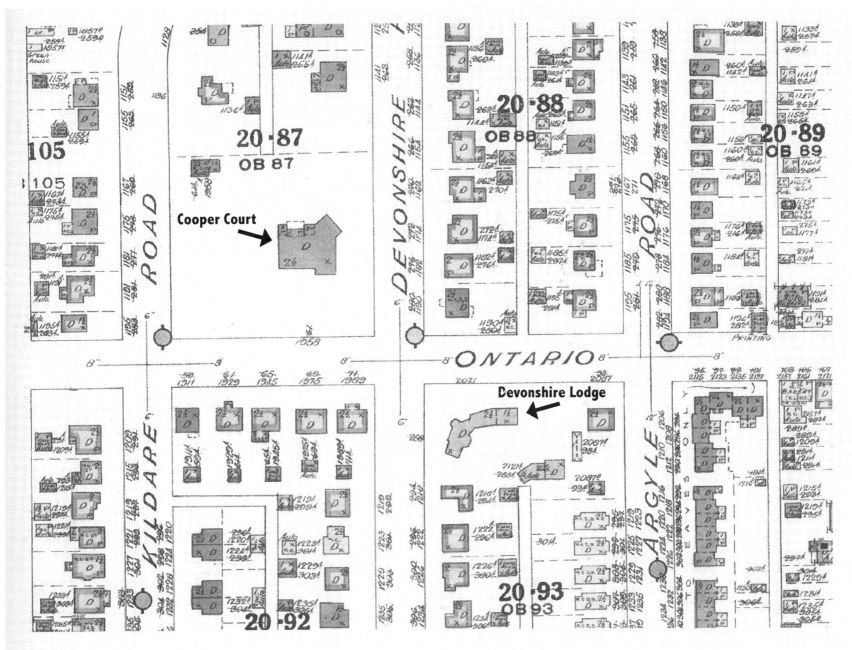

Fire Insurance Map, Windsor 1937

A fire insurance map from 1937 shows the relative positioning of Harry Low's Devonshire Lodge and James Cooper's Cooper Court. (Courtesy City of Windsor Geomatics Division)

Set amidst a neighbourhood of homes that were built facing their streets squarely, Low's house breaks the mould. Being set back from the street, on an angle, affords the house a greater level of prominence. You can quickly imagine through a brief glance at the 1937 fire insurance map for Walkerville what Harry Low had in mind when he sited his house in this manner.

Diagonally across from Low's creation, on the northwest corner of Devonshire and Ontario, and taking up the southern half of the entire block, sat Cooper Court, what was perhaps the largest and grandest home ever built in this region, arguably grander even than Willistead Manor and Amherstburg's Bellevue House. Low built his house facing Cooper Court, eye-to-eye. It is an in-your-face act, a bold statement of aggression toward his rival rumrunner, James Scott Cooper.

Cooper Court is gone now. Torn down by his widow after Cooper mysteriously disappeared off a ship in the middle of the Atlantic Ocean in February 1931, all that is left are the grand entry gates on Devonshire and Kildare roads, and the gatehouses. Low's house sits alone, the undisputed heavyweight champion of the corner.

Harry Low's house never aspired to be as grand as Cooper's. At 4,800 square feet, it is much smaller. And while its curved frontage rolls forward like a military incursion, the house is actually narrow, back to front. It's almost like a false front designed to hide the fact that it really isn't that large.

Grossi says the house breaks with a number of formalities and traditions. While it gives the appearance of a Cotswold style, it has a formal entry that no Cotswold would possess. "It's a deliberate attempt, I believe, to say, 'look at this site as being completely different'."

Once inside, the visitor enters the very centre of the house at the base of the grand walnut staircase. From this point, the home's private family areas are to the left, while the public areas lie to the right.

"Normally with a grand home, you are invited in and design-wise, it's considered whether you are worthy of coming in to the home, and only afterwards you are granted access and then the home starts to open itself up to you. This home is immediate. You are in and you are either going in to the public area or to the private area. I don't recall any other expression of that locally."

The house is neither elegant nor pretty in a traditional manner. And yet, along with Willistead, Devonshire Lodge creates Walkerville's "exclamation points," says Grossi. Other homes on the finer streets of Walkerville blend in. They are built in a similar fashion, sited along tree-lined streets.

He says historically, Devonshire Lodge is also significant because of the mystique that encases it. It is deeply immersed in the urban lore that is Walkerville and the rumrunners.

Others have tried to describe the eclectic house. One of the most interesting descriptions came in a report compiled for the Windsor Architectural Conservation Advisory Committee before former owner Paul Martin Sr. died in 1992. In that report, urban development expert James Yanchula called the house "a strong interpretation of the Picturesque mode of expression closely associated with the architectural tenets of the Arts and Crafts Movement."

Telling your muntins from your mullions: The mullion is the vertical or horizontal piece between adjoining window units. The muntin is the narrow strip dividing panes of glass.

But, he added, "the design is based primarily on the archetypal forms of 15th- and 16th-century peasant cottages found in the English countryside." Unlike its medieval inspiration, though, "this 'cottage' is clad in rusticated stone rather than whitewash." Another departure is the cylindrical turret with its conical roof and the use of curved glass.

Yanchula said the moulded wavy roofline was designed to resemble thatch from the medieval period, with the roof "rolling" over the eaves to complete the appearance. He called the leaded glass a departure from most of Walkerville's other examples of leaded glass, with the pattern created with the muntins and mullions "significantly artistic."

Inside, the house continues its unusual course. By the late 1920s, most new construction included indoor plumbing and one bathroom. Home and garden magazines that wrote of aspirational living noted the luxury of a second bathroom was creeping in to the finer homes. Harry Low built seven bathrooms in his house!

Each of the four upstairs bedrooms came with its own ensuite bath, each finished in a different colour of tile. Two of the bathrooms contained body showers, a luxury many dream of today.

The craftsmanship

Rusticated rough-cut stone was brought in for the construction of Devonshire Lodge by barge from Amherstburg. Stonecutters from Montreal were employed to create the unusual exterior walls.

Inside, the stonework continues, with Caen stone, a beautiful creamy French limestone quarried in northwest France near the town of Caen, used for

Intricate crown moulding designs in the dining room complement the rich wood panelling and walnut staircase.

the fireplace that is the focal point of the living room. Caen stone is employed in important cathedrals across Europe and is valued for being easy to carve. Did Low stand in awe of some of France's grand cathedrals on one of his European trips and imagine a bit of the same spirit in his own home?

The hardwood floors are both strip hardwood and parquet. In an era when parquet is pre-constructed and laid down in squares, the concept has lost some of its allure. When Vern Myslichuk first saw Devon-

Work proceeds on the walnut staircase during construction. The staircase has erroneously been described as oak, including in the ad on page 91. (Courtesy Jim Cooper)

shire Lodge's parquet, he assumed it had been put in during some latter-year renovation. Later, when he viewed photographs of the original home that were discovered during research for this book, he realized the work was original.

For many, it is hard to fathom that parquet was once the prerogative of only the wealthy. In those times, the individual pieces of wood were laid down in an intricate pattern and nailed to their backing. This is how Devonshire Lodge's parquet floors were created.

"Everything is face-nailed, it's not tongue-in-groove," Myslichuk says with admiration. "Each piece is face-nailed in. To install that would take forever."

Reportedly, specially skilled craftsmen were brought in from Europe to work on the interior construction. Andrew Ledoux of Ledoux Interiors does both new construction and restoration and says the original workmanship was "extremely well done." Ledoux and his father, Gerry, spent hundreds of hours restoring the interior stone and plasterwork and says the original plasterer was "obviously highly skilled."

Detailing in the crown moulding is "classical", says Ledoux, and popular in Detroit buildings of the early 1900s. He counted "15 or 16" different moulding details around the house. The ceiling tracery, however, is quite uncommon, he adds. "Each ceiling was a different layout. In terms of cost, today, that would be difficult."

The stunning staircase that rises from the centre of the house is a highlight of the mansion's interior. A photograph provided by Jim Cooper, son of the former Walkerville Lumber owner, proves it was "created" rather than simply manufactured – custom-built onsite. It shows two workmen standing at the base of the under-construction stairway, surrounded by open rafters and unfinished woodwork.

"I believe a lot of the wood that went into this house came from Walkerville Lumber," says Cooper.

The roof

Most agree the standout feature of the house is its roof. Even more so than the heavy rock façade and the almost chilling perseverance of the house on its corner, the roof makes the house unique.

It is reminiscent of both a rolling sea and a traditional thatch-roof cottage. The effect is particularly surprising when you realize the wavy lines were created through the actual structure of the roof framing, rather than being an optical illusion suggested by the overlapping and directional changes of the shingles.

These "wood thatch" roofs evolved from the popularity of English Tudor and cottage designs in the early part of the 20th century, according to Larry Jones of the Utah State Historical Society, who authored an article on the topic for The Old-House Journal in 1983. He said that by 1912, building magazines were showing examples of wood shingles designed to look like thatch.

Promoted by the Creo-Dipt Company of North Tonawanda, New York, the style was particularly popular in the 1920s and 1930s. Gables, eaves and valleys were rounded to accommodate cedar shingles that were bent at the time of manufacture.

According to an article from 1984 in Fine Homebuilding Magazine, builders would often send floor

The faux-thatched roof of cedar shingles sits on a frame structure that is made to resemble a rolling sea.

A full-page ad for King Greenhouses featuring Harry Low's new house appeared in the July 1928 edition of Canadian Homes & Gardens magazine.

plans and elevations to the Creo-Dipt company so engineers and designers could produce the necessary roof-framing plans. Shingles were even prestained with creosote as a preservative, with five shades offered.

Beneath the shingles, the framing was actually curved. Lumber and lath strips were bent to form the curved nailing surface onto which the shingles were placed. With the additional shingles needed to finish the effect, these roofs weighed 60 per cent more than traditional roofs and were far more costly to build.

Decades later, when it came time to replace these bent-shingle roofs, roofers invented steamers which they brought to the building site to bend the shingles. Once they were softened, the shingles were placed in a metal break, pressed and allowed to cool.

John Kitts of Windsor's Alternative Roofing was called in to consult on the roof in 2008 when Frank Vella owned the house. "The roof has always intrigued me", he says. "I'd never seen anything quite like it."

Kitts says an American expert they brought in to look at the roof was convinced it was the Creo-Dipt company that provided the original cedar shingles. He describes the framework beneath the shingles as resembling a series of "ski moguls" or bumps in the surface.

Once completed, the roof provided much-needed relief from the severity of the house's rusticated dark stone walls, a softening influence in an otherwise extravaganza of masculinity.

The garden

The yard and garden is another feature of Devonshire Lodge that sets it apart from the normal. Harry Low wanted a pasture-like front yard and had built what Margaret Lawton Spencer described as hillocks on the lawn to resemble a natural meadow or pasture, perhaps a further clue to his fascination with English country homes.

The garden adds to the Cotswold feel, says architect Jason Grossi. The "characteristic garden wall" is typical of a Cotswold property. He says the curved front wall of the house gives a contoured effect that is normal for cottage and farm homes from the Cotswold Hills region of west-central England. "My guess is that Harry Low went on a vacation and took some good pictures with his Brownie camera."

Grossi says Cotswold homes were "medieval" in their planning, with a central staircase that was located for security reasons. The head of the house would sleep at the foot of the stairs to interrupt intruders who might want to harm the family.

In his original construction of the house and garden, Low added a glass greenhouse that sat between the house and the garage/servants' quarters. This greenhouse was featured in a July 1928 advertisement for King Greenhouses and Conservatories that appeared in Canadian Homes & Gardens magazine.

Possibly the addition of the greenhouse was an idea that came from Harry's younger brother, Sam, who was known for his green thumb and in later years with Harry's financial backing, opened a greenhouse and flower business in his native Ottawa. The business, located not far from where the children of

Ford Motor Company of Canada used Devonshire Lodge for a photo shoot to show off the luxury of its 1929 Model A Sport Coupe.

Frank and Sarah Ann Low grew up, was called Rideau Flowers.

The greenhouse and magazine feature were not the only photo shoots ever undertaken at Harry Low's newly built creation. Former owner Frank Vella was at work on the house after buying it in 2008 when he came upon a fascinating artifact from the house's early days.

"I was doing some renovation work and hidden behind a wall we found negatives of when Ford did a photo shoot," he says. The photos show a 1929 Ford Model A Sport Coupe.

The coachhouse, showing the drive-through garage on the right. To the left of the coachhouse sits the former greenhouse. (Canadian Homes & Gardens)

Leaded glass doors, pastel coloured bath tiles (these are pink) and intricate custom outdoor wall sconces helped to define Devonshire Lodge.

Devonshire Lodge at a glance

- Construction: 1927-28
  Builder/designer: George Lawton
  Exterior: Rough-cut stone
  Roof: Wavy gable style, cedar shingle
  Other highlights include: One hip-style wavy dormer; tower with turret; many crystal windows and stained glass windows; spiral walnut staircase; drip plaster ceilings; walnut wall panels
- Quick description: Rusticated stone English cottage or Cotswold style house, the only one of this style in the city and perhaps the county. Its convex façade consists of numerous bays with elements such as jerkinhead gables, conical roof over the rounded bay, a recessed balconette over the arched recessed entrance, leaded glass and oriel windows.
  (A jerkinhead gable is a gable end that slopes back at the top to form a hipped roof end. An oriel window is a bay-style window that does not extend to the ground.)
- The roof is characterized by shingles that roll over the eaves. Originally, the undulating roof consisted of four layers of wafer thin wooden shingles and laid over a complex wooden framework. In the 1960s, Paul and Nellie Martin replaced the roof with asphalt shingles in layers in an attempt to simulate the rolled appearance.
- The garage/servants' apartment is built in the same style.
- A garden wall and a winding stone path that leads to the main entrance.

A City of Windsor report says the house "is one of Windsor's most important, beautiful and recognized homes, a heritage landmark in the former town of Walkerville, one of the last remaining 19th century garden/company towns left in the world. ... (The house) is one of the finest estate homes built during Walkerville's later stages of development."

Factors that contribute to its historical value

- Its association with Harry Low
- Its association with Paul Martin Sr.
- Its association with visits by prime ministers Lester B. Pearson and Pierre Trudeau.
- Its association with builder George Lawton
- Its rare English Cotswold style
- Its estate status with crescent-shaped main house
- Original landscape elements, including the rear garden wall and winding stone path
- Overall quality of construction of rusticated stone with limestone trim, decorative wooden elements and copper eaves and downspouts
- Its undulating roof that emulates thatch
- Architectural elements including asymmetrical bays, recessed balconette over the arched recessed entranceway and oriel windows with leaded bevelled glass
- Recessed arched stone main entrance with ornate arched wooden door
- Leaded bevelled glass windows
- Its site configuration resulting in unobstructed views of the prominent main house on the southeast corner of Ontario and Devonshire

Walnut wall panels and stained glass windows are among the features that highlight the interior.

In May 2008, Jason Grossi wrote Windsor's heritage committee in support of an application for public funds to help in the immense job of preserving the house from further decay. Of its significance, he wrote: "Its architectural style is definitely from some outside source and is truly unique to this region, resembling the work of architect Harold Zook or Van Doren Shaw from Illinois, perhaps."

(Courtesy Jim Cooper)

Chapter 5:

The Downfall of Harry Low

WITH RAGE ETCHING HIS FACE, Harry Low raised the chair high in the air and brought it down so hard it smashed the glass table in the boardroom of Carling Breweries. Things hadn't been going well for Low and his colleagues. By 1930, federal authorities were increasingly after the various companies he had created for unpaid taxes. The U.S. border patrol was employing thousands of machine-gun-wielding police officers in its crackdown on shipments from Canada and Low's own federal government had agreed to help them out. Low stood and surveyed the shattered table. He wondered where things had all started to go so wrong.

Probably it had been those damned feds when they set up the Royal Commission in 1926 to investigate the payment, or, more to the point, the non-payment of customs and excise taxes owed to them by the country's brewers and distillers. Then there had been the murder of the Carling accountant, Jack Kennedy – a murder for which Low had been a suspect although never charged – and the kidnapping of Low's own brother, Sam, by hoodlums unknown.

As well as their problems with two federal governments, the province of Ontario had begun to foul things up for the rumrunners by legalizing the sale of alcohol again, an act that had cut deeply into the revenues of Harry Low and Company. Their bills were up and their revenues were down. Why was everyone out to get Harry Low? Where was it all going to end?

Life at Devonshire Lodge

Harry and Nellie Low had been anticipating the move to Devonshire Lodge for a very long time. On that early summer day in 1928 when they moved in, they still had every reason to believe their lives there would be happy and their stay would be long. But it was not to be. Even as they took possession of their newly built Walkerville mansion, the family was reeling from the kidnapping and murder of a long-time employee of Carling Breweries, John Allen Kennedy. Within days, it was being whispered in police

WINDSOR MAN FOUND SLAIN NEAR TOLEDO

John A. Kennedy Was Once Interested In Liquor Trade

POLICE PROBE CASE

"Feud" Hinted in Death Of Border Resident; Was Drugged, Belief

All the law forces of the Dominion and Ontario, co-operating with Michigan State police and Windsor detectives, were turned loose today to track down the slayers of John A. Kennedy, well-known Windsor man, who was "taken for a ride" and slain near Toledo, Ohio.

TORONTO AIR MAIL SERVICE STARTED

Soon after Carling bookkeeper John Allen Kennedy was killed in what appeared to be a mob hit, rumours circulated that Harry Low was involved.

circles that Harry Low was the likely figure behind it. Throughout the summer the whispers grew louder and spilled onto the streets of the Border Cities.

In February 1928, the Royal Commission on Customs and Excise had reported its findings and presented a long list of incidents of bribery, forgery, bootlegging and smuggling laid at the steps of Low and his colleagues. The Globe newspaper had then called bootlegging Windsor's basic industry, "raised to the dignity of a profession." Law-abiding citizens were outraged by rumors that exporters such as Low were using bribes and fines for liquor violations as income tax deductions.

Then, no sooner had Harry and Nellie settled comfortably in to the magnificent new home than Harry's own brother, Sam, had been kidnapped and held for ransom. It so unsettled the family that they decided their children, Norah and Frank, would be driven to school by an armed chauffeur.

Despite their troubles, Harry and Nellie were determined to enjoy their home. They opened their door to a reporter and photographer who had come to do a feature article for the magazine Canadian Homes & Gardens, which appeared in the February 1929 edition. This is how the article described their home:

Textured wall finishes have been used almost entirely throughout Mr. Low's home. The dining room has walls finished in antiqued ivory, making a suitable background for the rose and blue tones of the Chinese rug, for the tapestry upholstered chairs and the large pieces of walnut, ornamented with black and gold lacquering.

The living room also has used ivory textured walls, enlivening them with panels of crimson brocade. Persian rugs are used on the floor and in the upholstered pieces and in the hangings, green has been favoured. A Caen stone fireplace brings a note of distinction into the room. A small conservatory, with a blue and terra cotta-tiled floor, is glimpsed in the centre view, and a sunroom, furnished in wicker, is seen.

The story went on to detail the master bedroom, which was done in mauve and gold, the adjoining bathroom repeating the theme. "The guest room is in shot green and taffeta, with soft touches of salmon pink."

The piazza was "low and hospitable … shielded by a gay striped awning."

The shingles, said the story, "have been stained soft colours in random effect, thereby supplying the necessary light note above the grey stone walls of the building." The roof treatment was called the outstanding feature and "simulates Old Country thatching." The recessed balcony with overhanging roof over the entrance suggested 16th-century England, "with more than a hint of medieval expansiveness."

Photographs accompanying the story revealed a Heintzman baby grand piano in a corner of the living room, wall sconces and chandeliers, wall tapestries and artwork, and even a fountain in the conservatory. A full-sized Venus de Milo sat nearby.

It seemed to be a home that longed for parties. And yet by all reports, Harry Low guarded his privacy jealously and maintained a strict boundary between his private family life and his life as a high-stakes businessman whose chosen occupation kept him skirting the laws of his own land, and shattering those of the United States.

One of the few times they'd opened up their home to a large gathering had been the year before they moved in to Devonshire Lodge, when they still lived in the yellow brick house half a block north. It had been the occasion of the marriage of Harry's brother, Syd, to Eva May Hackney. Harry must have looked on proudly at his wife and daughter, whose outfits garnered special mention in the newspaper account of the wedding.

"Mrs. Harry Low and her daughter, Miss Norah Low, were in smart French imports of black satin, with touches of pink and chic hats," reported the newspaper, clearly differentiating their attire from the more staid "grey georgette" and "blue crepe" of the other women in attendance.

"After the ceremony, a reception followed at the home of Mr. and Mrs. Harry Low, Devonshire Road, Walkerville," continued the article.

The next summer, once they were living at Devonshire Lodge, Harry and Nellie usually limited their entertaining to close friends and family, or occasionally a business associate. One such associate was a frequent visitor from Chicago who would drop by for a quiet drink once his business dealings with Low were completed. After the visitor exchanged pleasantries with Nellie, he and Harry would normally slip away to the basement bar for a stiff libation and some serious business conversation.

The visitor's name was Al Capone. Capone was a ruthless gangster, wise enough to not cross the even more ruthless Detroiters known as the Purple Gang. Rather than fight them, Capone chose to do business in compliance with their wishes, to ensure a steady supply of beverages into his Midwestern haunts. It was a practice that frequently brought him to the Canadian side of the river, to the giant supplier, Harry Low.

Photos of the dining room and living room appear in the February 1929 edition of Canadian Homes & Gardens. The dining room suite is one of just four ever produced.

The piazza, far left, is covered by a striped awning. At left, another view of the living room shows the parquet flooring and panels of crimson brocade hanging on the walls.

Years later, Nellie Low would occasionally speak of Capone's visits during conversations with her grandson, Bruce. "She said that he was at the house many times and that he was one of the nicest guys she'd ever met," Bruce Low says. "A real gentleman, she said. She was impressed that he never swore or anything like that. I guess he was an all-round great guy – until you crossed him."

Did Harry Low and Al Capone ever compare stories of their respective troubles? If so, Low might have mentioned that 1928 was turning in to a particularly troubling year. Besides the problems associated with the findings of the Canadian Royal Commission, in May, Kennedy's body was discovered.

A longtime bookkeeper for Carling, Kennedy had left the company and gone on an extended vacation about the same time the federal Royal Commission wished to question him about his signature on a number of suspicious cheques. The fact of his vacation was itself a bit of a mystery: How could a man living on an accountant's modest wage afford such a luxurious trip? Rumors circulated the trip had been conveniently scheduled for Kennedy by his Carling employers.

Eventually, he returned and Kennedy was subpoenaed to testify in Toronto on May 7, 1928. He is reported to have told friends, "I'm sick of all the lying and subterfuge. I'm going to tell them what I know."

A week before he was to appear at the hearings, Kennedy disappeared from his Windsor apartment. Four days later, a group of children discovered his body in dense woods north of Toledo. While the investigation involved police forces from both countries and continued for months, there were never any arrests. Whoever was responsible had covered their tracks effectively.

Weeks after the Kennedy murder, Low's hometown newspaper hailed the announcement of the huge Dominion Square real estate deal in Montreal and proudly played up the Border Cities connection. It would be the last time Harry Low was treated with such admiration by the newspaper. Days later, Low and his partners were caught up in the raids on the export docks and the daring car-in-the-river stunt that followed. Afterwards, the newspaper changed its tone dramatically.

With rumors about a potential Low connection to the Kennedy slaying deepening, the Border Cities Star ran an editorial excoriating the "shameful" business of the region's liquor barons. Clearly, circumstances were eating away at Low's reputation.

Low and his partners were given short shrift in the newspaper when they announced details of plans for their downtown Windsor office building a few days later. It was to be built by the same Windsor "syndicate" that had announced the Montreal project, the Border Cities Star reported simply, with no reference to Low by name. Windsorites were highly familiar with the term "syndicate" to describe the notorious Chicago gangsters who toiled for Al Capone.

The newspaper's intentions seemed clear. Almost overnight, Harry Low had turned from hero to zero. Things would only get worse.

The Border Cities Star reports on the kidnapping of Harry Low's brother, Sam, in September 1928

Kidnapping

On the night of September 10, 1928, Sam Low was driving, alone, along Highway 2 between Windsor and London. Just after he passed Thamesville in his sporty roadster, a large sedan pulled up alongside him and forced him to the side of the road. Four armed men jumped out of the pursuing vehicle, a flashlight was shone into Low's face and he was ordered, at gunpoint, out of the car. Handcuffs were snapped on him and a blindfold was placed over his eyes.

Two men led Low to the larger car and drove off into the night, the others following in Sam Low's own roadster. They drove to the Kingsville area and took their hostage to a cottage on the lake. Low was laid out on a bed and secured to its posts. Then the men sat down next to him for a talk.

A ransom figure of $500,000 was mentioned.

Calmly, Sam Low told the men this would be an unlikely sum but that if they contacted Carling's lawyer, Major James H. Clark, back in Windsor, more modest arrangements might be made. Low noticed that two pieces of paper the men handed him on which to write their demands had each come from a different Detroit hotel, which would later be considered clues to their identity. He was told they were demanding ransom of $35,000, considerably less than their original figure.

Still blindfolded, Low was escorted to his own car, placed in the passenger seat and driven in to Windsor where he was dropped off on Ouellette Avenue and told to deliver his own ransom note to Major Clark. This is where the official police record seems to diverge from reality.

The official report is that no ransom was ever paid. But over the next few years, a much different

Harry and Nellie Low insisted their daughter, Norah, and son, Frank, be driven to school by an armed chauffeur after Sam Low's kidnapping. (Courtesy Bruce Low)

story surfaced. While speaking in 1934 of the John S. Labatt kidnapping, Detroit police chief of detectives Fred W. Frahm revealed that $30,000 had been paid for Sam Low's release.

In 1936, the figure was reported as $33,000 as police sought to find a link between the two kidnappings. That same newspaper report claimed further evidence in Sam Low's ordeal indicated he was tortured and at one time was buried to his neck in sand as Lake Erie's waves crashed overtop of him.

The family said little of the matter in public. Bruce Low says he was told years later that his grandfather, Harry, personally paid $35,000 for Sam's release. Bruce Low says his Uncle Sam was so shaken by the ordeal that Harry sent him on a long worldwide cruise to recuperate and afterwards sent him to Ottawa and set him up in the flower business.

So who was responsible for Sam Low's kidnapping, and why? The modis operandi in the kidnappings of Sam Low and John Labatt were nearly identical. Both men were pulled over by a pursuing vehicle while driving alone on a secluded stretch of highway. Both were abducted at gunpoint, blindfolded and taken to a lonely cottage and secured to a bed where the terms of release were dictated. Both were forced to write ransom notes. In both cases, the abductees were released on a city street.

Those believed involved in, and convicted of the Labatt kidnapping were small-time hoods and gamblers. No one was ever brought to trial in the Sam Low incident. Bruce Low says he grew up on the story that it had been Detroit's Purple Gang who nabbed his uncle, the same Purple Gang that had introduced Harry Low to the big leagues of liquor export. Certainly, the writing paper from two Detroit hotels would support that thought. Had Harry done something to displease them?

Perhaps it's more likely that the same small-time hoodlums who botched the Labatt kidnapping had tried the same thing more than five years earlier. The real story will likely never be known.

(As an addendum to the story, it later came to light that Harry Low's partner, Charles Burns, the former Carling president, was also kidnapped in 1933.)

Legal troubles

Harry Low continued to carry on business with his partners, Leon and Burns. Under the name LL & B Distilleries, they bought an old abattoir and announced plans to turn it into a distillery, which was likely their first foray into the alcohol production business beyond brewing. They continued to buy and sell real estate in Windsor and Toronto.

But their legal problems grew. With the report of the royal commission, government prosecutors were starting to move against brewers, distillers and exporters. The national revenue department opened a case against Carling Export Brewing and Malting in April 1929, arguing that beer intended for export had actually been short-circuited back to Canada and not properly taxed. Carling called upon "an imposing array of legal talent" to prove its innocence of allegations, reported the Border Cities Star. Low lost and the government told his firm: "pay up."

In 1930, the U.S. beefed up its border patrol along the Detroit/Windsor border, armed 10,000 men with machine-guns and announced it would "shoot to kill" any rumrunners. Under this growing pressure,

The Detroit River is crucial to Harry Low's success but proves to represent increasingly troubled waters as the 1920s come to an end. (Library of Congress)

Extradition Of Harry Low Is Ordered Today

Windsor Man Wanted in U.S. For Alleged Bribery Of Customs Official, Will Appeal Again.

Hon. Mr. Justice Logie in weekly court this morning dismissed a motion for discharge on the return of a writ of habeas corpus requiring Harry Low, of Windsor, to report for extradition to the United States. Low is wanted in the United States on a charge of bribing a United States customs officer.

Charge Harry Low In Registration Of Stocks in N. York

Associated Press

NEW YORK, Aug. 26.—Harry Low, of suburban Detroit and Ormond Beach, Fla., a Canadian seeking United States citizenship, was arrested here late yesterday on a charge of withholding a material fact in seeking registration of stocks in the now closed Trenton Valley Distillers Corp., Trenton, Mich., of which he is former

Bail for Harry Low Being Asked by Counsel

Application for bail is being made this afternoon for Harry Low, Windsor, Ont., arrested yesterday for the United States authorities on a charge of bribing a U.S. customs officer. Bail was refused yesterday by Judge Daly. Royden Hughes is making the second application

APRIL 25, 1933.

Judgment Tells Why Harry Low Given Freedom

U.S. Failed to Show Alleged Acts of Bribery Offences Against Laws, Says Chief Justice Mulock.

(Canadian Press.)

TORONTO, April 24.—"In order to be entitled to extradition of the accused it was necessary for the United States to prove that, at the

Harry Low's legal problems mount during the early 1930s.

CATALOGUE

AUCTION SALE

OF

HANDSOME HOUSE FURNISHINGS AND PALATIAL HOME

Known as the
DEVONSHIRE LODGE
Corner of Devonshire Road and Ontario Streets
Walkerville, Ont.

Belonging to
MR. HARRY M. LOW

Will be Sold Without Reserve

Wednesday and Thursday
November 7th and 8th

Afternoons 3 p.m.   -   Evenings 8 p.m.

T. F. RYAN & S. H. LYON

AUCTIONEERS

House Open for Exhibition
TUESDAY, 10 a.m. till 10 p.m.
WEDNESDAY, 10 a.m. till time of Sale

the Canadian government imposed a crackdown on liquor shipments bound for the U.S., thus shutting down most of the export docks along the riverfront. Later that year, Low and his partners sold Carling to E.P. Taylor's liquor empire, Canadian Brewers Ltd., for a fraction of what it had been worth two years earlier.

Low was arrested at his Walkerville home in early 1931 and charged with conspiracy to smuggle whisky from Halifax to Windsor in railroad cars labelled "fresh fish." When taken to Halifax for trial, an indignant Low told the courtroom all he was trying to do was "feed a little rum to Americans." After all, he said, "their mouths are always open." He was acquitted of all charges but later convicted and sentenced to six months in jail for false billing of beer destined for export to the U.S.

An accusation that he bribed a U.S. customs officer led to an application from Washington for extradition. Faced with mounting bills and legal problems, on June 29, 1931, Harry and Nellie Low took out a mortgage on Devonshire Lodge in the amount of $20,000.

Because of his growing problems with the law, it's not surprising that Low seemed to be trying to change his image. In the late 1920s, he had listed himself in the municipal directory as manager and vice-president of Carling Breweries, even though his business connections went much farther. In the 1931 directory, however, Low indicated real estate was his business. The following year, he listed no career.

Low successfully fought the extradition, but his empire was crumbling. In April 1934, Harry and Nellie defaulted on the mortgage they had taken out on their home and relinquished their claim to it. The house fell into the hands of the mortgage holder, London insurance broker Philip Pocock. Faced with the inevitable, the Lows organized an auction sale of their belongings with the Toronto auction house of Ryan and Lyon. With Pocock's endorsement, the house itself was included.

The auction was held in November 1934. The newspaper ad read: "Handsome house furnishings and palatial home known as The Devonshire Lodge. Belonging to Mr. Harry M. Low, who is leaving Canada to reside in the United States." (No legal record ever listed a middle name for Harry, and this is the only reference to even a middle initial. It's difficult to speculate where the "M" came from or even why, now, in Low's darkest hour.)

Among the items offered were many rare and valuable pieces and included walnut and mahogany furniture, the baby grand piano and a player piano, Persian and Chinese rugs, gold-plated fireplace andirons and firebox, marble figures, silk drapes, tapestries, an Italian fountain, oil paintings and watercolours, Dresden lamps and Doulton vases.

Before the auction could be held, the federal government attempted to seize the contents to cover Low's debts and sent in the sheriff to halt the proceedings. The Lows were incensed and contacted their lawyer, Paul Martin Sr. of Martin and Laird, to obtain a writ, claiming that despite the wording of the ad and auction pamphlet, the contents were actually held in the name of Nellie Low. The auction proceeded.

While the contents were valued at $40,000, bidding was subdued and the Lows collected a paltry portion of that amount. As for the property, de-

CATALOGUE

Auction Sale

—of the—

HANDSOME HOUSE FURNISHINGS

AND

PALATIAL HOME

Known as
THE DEVONSHIRE LODGE
Corner of Devonshire Road and Ontario, St., WALKERVILLE, ONT.

Belonging to
MR. HARRY M. LOW
Who is leaving Canada to reside in the United States
Will be sold without reserve

WEDNESDAY AND THURSDAY
November 7th and 8th
Afternoon at 3 p.m.—Evenings at 8 p.m.

Handsome Carved Walnut Dining Room Suite, Michael Angelo Design, 12 Pieces, shown at the Wembley Exhibition, London, England, cost $8,000; 4 Master Bedroom Suites, Carved Walnut, three suites have Twin Beds, one cost $3,000; Heintzman Baby Grand Piano; Royal Tabriz Persian Rug, 12'6"x9'3"; Royal Kermanshah Rug, 15'x9', 12'x6', and 12'x15'; four Handsome Chinese Rugs, different colors, 9'x12'; nine Persian Scatter Rugs, 5'x3' and 6'x3'; Gheelem Rug, 6'x4'6"; Red Broadloom Carpet and Stair Runner; English Down Chesterfield and Chair; 3 French Gold Chairs; 4 Upholstered and Carved Walnut Arm Chairs; Carved Italian Walnut Table; 8 Smoke Stands, different styles; Gold Plated Andirons, and Fire Box; 2 Carved Carrara Marble Figures, one Life Size of Venus de Milo, cost One Thousand Dollars, one "The Three Graces," cost $500; Handsome French Silk Window Drapes in all rooms, different sizes, colors and materials, also Silk Marquisette Curtains; Rose Wicker Sunroom Suite, 6 pieces; Marconi Radio Combination; Mahogany Grandfather Chime Clock; Beautiful Table and Floor Lamps; Antique Sheffield Tea Set; 3 Pairs Excellent Cut Glass Decanters; Cloisonne, French Serves and Doulton Vases; Italian Marble Fountain with Birds; Walnut Fenery; Walnut Desk; Carved Walnut Hall Chair; Excellent Oil Paintings and Water Colors; Player Piano; Dresden Lamps; 2 Chaise Longues silk covering; 12 Bathroom Mats; Carved Walnut Arm Chair; Aubusson Tapestry Covering; 2 Walnut Settees; Bronze Figures and Flower Pots. Numerous other articles.

THE PALATIAL STONE HOUSE, 3-CAR GARAGE
AND HELPS' LIVING APARTMENTS
AND GROUNDS
Will Be Offered

THURSDAY AFTERNOON AT 4 P.M.

All the above on Exhibition TUESDAY, NOVEMBER 6TH, 10 A.M. TILL 10 P.M. and on WEDNESDAY until time of sale. Catalogues on Application at House.

Sale conducted by
S. HOWARD LYON, Windsor Auctioneer
and
T. F. RYAN of Ryan's Art Galleries Limited, Toronto.

At left, the cover from the auction brochure for the house and furnishings. Above, the ad that ran in the Border Cities Star.

scribed as a "palatial stone house, three-car garage, helps' living apartments and grounds", there were just two bids on the first day, one of $15,000 and another of $20,000. Harry Low had spent $130,000 to build the home and the auctioneer's reserve bid was set at $182,000. At the end of the second day, the auctioneer reopened bidding on the house and asked for a bid of $25,000. There were no takers and the auctioneer lowered his ask to $20,000.

Silence. The house did not sell.

Farewell to Windsor

After leaving Devonshire Lodge, Harry and Nellie left the Border Cities behind and moved across the river where they lived for a time at the Fort Shelby Hotel in Detroit. Later, they moved to Ormond Beach, Florida.

While he stumbled financially, Low's ideas never failed him. If the liquor business was faltering, there were other ways to earn a living. He had invested in numerous stocks, including uranium mines, which tumbled in value in the 1929 market crash. He became a promoter, a real estate investor and even an inventor. His invention was called the More Miles Carburetor, and he even set up a factory in Tilbury to manufacture it. In an era when fuel was cheap, the auto industry was cool to the idea, although it is believed Low received a handsome payment from a consortium of oil companies that conveniently sent the idea to the scrap heap.

He joined a group of Lambton County oilmen to finance a scheme to use hydraulic fracturing to capture crude from old played-out wells. He proposed re-establishing a wine industry on Pelee Island where the first industry had died out some years earlier. Interestingly, just as with his carburetor, these ideas had merit but seemed to have come at the wrong time. While secondary crude extraction is now widely accepted procedure and Pelee Island Winery has been operating since 1980, Harry Low didn't live to see his ideas to fruition.

In 1933, the United States repealed Prohibition and the production and sale of alcoholic beverages was once again legal across the land. If Harry Low could no longer benefit from the illegality of alcohol, he decided he might as well try making some money from its new-found legality. In 1934, he partnered with a group to establish the Trenton Valley Distillers Corp. of Trenton, Michigan. For his free-wheeling days as the baron of booze, Low was rewarded with the position of president.

However, in August that year things began to go sour. Low was charged with stock manipulation for trying to take an option on 45,000 shares in Trenton Valley Distillers before it was registered, and failing to reveal this fact. Then, hobbled by a lack of working capital from the start, the distillery was shuttered in 1937.

Low petitioned to become a naturalized American citizen in 1936, but his nefarious past caught up to him. Claims were pending for the non-payment of hundreds of thousands of dollars in taxes to the Canadian government. The old partners Low, Leon and Burns, joined by Nellie Low as a fellow director, had formed the E.B.M. Company in a desperate attempt to avoid their huge tax bill. E.B.M., formerly the Carling Export Brewing and Malting Company and then Carling Breweries Ltd., appealed the tax

Al Capone: Born in Brooklyn, Capone earned his reputation and his wealth in Chicago. He revelled in the adulation he earned from the down-and-out Depression-era populace who saw him as a modern-day Robin Hood for his frequent charitable donations. Arrested in 1931, he was convicted of tax evasion and spent eight years behind bars.

bill but the manoeuvre failed.

Low was arrested in 1937 in New York on charges of income tax evasion and indicted the following year. Interestingly, the allegations hinted that Low was far from broke during the mid-1930s at least. Income obtained in the United States amounted to more than $30,000 in 1935 and more than $23,000 the next year, the charges said. Those were handsome sums in the midst of the Great Depression. Additional charges were laid for using the mails to defraud in connection with the stock deals.

Released on $5,000 bond in 1939, Low disappeared, headed back to Canada and moved with his wife, daughter and grandson to Sorel, Quebec, where again he took up his tool and die trade, this time at the Sorel shipyards, which built many of the vessels for Canada's Second World War naval fleet.

In 1947, while still living in Sorel, Low partnered with a group to establish a brewery in Tecumseh, Ontario's old Dominion Cannery. The building had begun life as a brewery under the Tecumseh Beer and Ale label and now it would reopen as Old Comrades Brewing. Operations began in August 1948 and it was sold to Canadian Breweries in 1952, and closed four years later.

Under the alias of Harry Love, in 1949 Low took his family back to Grosse Pointe, Michigan, and got work as a tool and die maker. He lived there in one of that community's first townhouses, for a time quietly beneath the radar of U.S. federal authorities.

Then in December 1953, FBI agents came knocking at the door and arrested him on the old charges of stock swindling and tax evasion. A Windsor Star headline reported: "Windsor millionaire of 1930s, broke, faces swindle, tax evasion charges." Low told authorities he had been living in the city for the past five years and working as a toolmaker.

His true identity came to light only when he attempted to establish his own tool and die business under the name Harry Love. One story has it that someone caught a glimpse of him in an old photograph. Another version is that a former business associate sold him out for the reward.

When asked to explain his disappearance 14 years earlier, there were signs of the old Harry Low flair. Low insisted he told U.S. authorities back in 1939 he was going to Windsor. When he didn't hear anything from them, he assumed "influential friends" had "taken care" of his case. A newspaper account described the defendant as "well dressed and living in a new apartment." However, Low told the judge he was unable to raise the $10,000 bail set for his release.

In 1954, Low was sentenced to a year and a day incarceration. He was told that he could avoid that prison time if he agreed to deportation to Canada. Low jumped at the opportunity and moved back to Windsor, into a home at 272 McKay Street, just north of University Avenue. He was back in the old haunts, not far from where he and Nellie had begun their lives in the Border Cities 35 years before.

There he lived in a neat and clean little home with wife Nellie, their daughter, Norah, and her son, Bruce.

Life with grandpa

Bruce Low was born in 1941. His mother was Norah, the only daughter, and one of two children born to Harry and Nellie Low. When he was young,

Sorel shipbuilding: Marine Industries of Sorel was instrumental in fitting the Royal Canadian Navy during the Second World War. It delivered 30 Liberty ships as well as light frigates, minesweepers, troop carrier barges and fleet oilers.

Harry Low with grandson Bruce in Sorel, Quebec.

After losing the house, Harry and Nellie lived for a time in Ormond Beach, Florida.

From left, son Frank, Nellie, Harry, daughter Norah and grandson Bruce Low.

Harry Low with Frank's daughter, Debbie.

When he died on August 21, 1955, Harry Low was living in a house on McKay Street in Windsor.

Harry and Nellie (Norah) Low are buried in Windsor Grove Cemetery. (Photos courtesy Bruce Low)

Bruce's parents' marriage broke up and Harry and Nellie opened their doors to Norah and Bruce. He recalls living in Sorel, Grosse Pointe and then Windsor, as well as spending a few of his early years in Tilbury, Ontario, likely with his mother's brother, Frank. Harry and Nellie adopted their grandson so that he could grow up with the name "Low," a name Bruce carries proudly to this day.

Bruce Low recalls his grandfather as a gentle man who never swore at home and who always had kind words for his family. At every mealtime, Harry would compliment Nellie on "the best meal he'd ever had." He would take one drink a day – a shot of rum in some milk – before going to bed. "Doctor's orders," Bruce recalls. The man who earned a fortune producing and peddling alcohol was for much of his life only a moderate drinker himself.

Bruce remembers the move to Sorel and one time, a trip in to Montreal with his grandfather in connection with business pertaining to the troublesome Dominion Square. A settlement of ownership issues left Low with a small fraction of the money he believed was owed to him.

When Bruce and his mother moved back with Harry and Nellie to Grosse Pointe, they lived in a brand new townhouse. Bruce was 12 when the FBI came knocking at the door to arrest his grandfather.

His grandfather might have lost his fortune, says Bruce, but never his pride. "He smiled a lot. Seemed relaxed, always at ease, content. On top of the world. Never an argument in our house. Never an ill word. I guess we were considered poor, but I never knew it."

Bruce recounts how one time when as a boy he desperately wanted a bicycle, his grandfather sold some of his tools to pay for one. "He nearly cried doing it."

And while Bruce remembers his grandfather as a calm, even-tempered man, he does recount one incident at the Grosse Pointe tool and die shop that made him realize Harry had a temper. One of the staff had done something harebrained and Harry railed on about it. "He swore pretty good that time. First time I ever heard him swear."

Gord Low is 11 years older than Bruce, and a son of Harry's brother, Syd. He, too, has fond memories of his Uncle Harry. "He was always into something," says Gord. "He would lose his money but he'd never give up."

It's Gord Low's recollection that it was only when "Harry Love" went to pick up the paperwork for the tool and die shop he wished to open, "that's when he was caught." Gord remembers going with his father to Detroit to bail out his uncle.

He also recalls Harry as a man with a constant stream of ideas. "He had a patent on the More Miles Carburetor and tried to sell stock and open up a plant. It never got off the ground."

"It was my dad (Syd) who gave Uncle Harry's house the nickname of Harry's rockpile," he laughs. "I was told all the stone was brought up from Amherstburg by barge. Some of the interiors and furnishings were imported from Europe."

Syd and his wife, Eva, lived for years in a Walkerville house on Chilver Road, which in those days was called Victoria Road. Gord says after they left Windsor, Harry and Nellie would come to their home for visits.

"My dad always said Uncle Harry was a little crazy. He and Aunt Norah (Nellie) lived in Florida for a while and I think they ran a goat farm. They'd come and visit and be all tanned. The family always said he became a millionaire again, after he lost it all. But then he lost that again. Dad said Harry would be driving around in a cab and take a shine to a piece of real estate and he'd buy it on the spot. He had more guts than Dick Tracy!

"Harry loved big cars and he drove them fast. He was always jovial, always selling something. He was a risk taker. A real likeable guy. Aunt Norah was quite small and she always stood in the background."

In the summer of 1955, Low took sick and was taken to Hotel-Dieu Hospital in Windsor where, on Sunday, August 21, 1955, he died.

Brothers Sam and Syd made the funeral arrangements. While the brothers had gone their separate ways, they were there for Harry just as they had been throughout his life, says Gord. The brothers were pallbearers at the service. Harry was buried at Windsor Grove Cemetery on Giles Boulevard. A simple red granite stone marks his grave next to Nellie, who died in 1988 at the age of 100. Of her husband the obituary read simply: "Beloved wife of the late Harry Low."

Harry Low did not spend his final days, as some reports had it, in "the shabby outcast" of a house on Pitt Street, an area then known as the hangout for "bootleggers, prostitutes, thieves, smugglers and killers." Nor did he live the "hand-to-mouth existence" that was also claimed. He did not end his days in "the grimy home of a jobless drifter."

Instead, he lived a quiet and comfortable existence back in the city where he had once made an immense fortune and built a house that shouted his success. Like others of his era, he applied an entrepreneur's spirit to the peculiar laws of the day.

Purged of notoriety

By the time of Low's death, his Walkerville monster of a mansion had been purged of its notorious beginnings through the transition of ownership. Windsor, too, had undergone a transition and the generation of the 1950s was not interested in being reminded of the mobsters, the rumrunners and the violence that had marked its history two and three decades before.

In April 1956, however, a man named Tom Butson penned a memoir of Low's life that for a brief moment reminded the world of the times that Harry Low had lived through and helped to shape. "There is no doubt that Harry Low was tough," wrote Butson. "In such company as he faced he had to be. Men like Capone and the (Purple Gang's) Licavolis fought dirtily for the forbidden grapes of Prohibition. Low had to fight back."

In those days, wrote Butson, "hijackers prowled like jackals on the fringes of the riverfront. Nosy U.S. customs agents and officials had to be reckoned with. The years of dodging the law took their toll on Harry Low. He was a tired old man when he came back to Windsor for the last time."

When Harry Low died, it was truly the end of an era and "the greatest racketeer of the hectic, tragic bootleg era had passed away quietly."

Chapter 6:

A Succession of Owners

THE ASSEMBLAGE OF ANTIQUES, collectibles and furniture – a house full of memorabilia obtained during their happier days together – slipped through the fingers of Harry and Nellie Low during the auction held at Devonshire Lodge over two days in November 1934. The loss of the items, gone at a fraction of their declared value, was the ultimate insult and hung as a ghostly reminder of Low's fall from grace.

The whereabouts of most of these items, scattered to the winds as buyers gathered in search of bargains, is no longer known. Many likely reside now in homes throughout the Windsor/Detroit area, their modern-day owners in many cases unaware of their provenance. Others would have made their way to antique dealers and consignment shops, resold to those who know nothing of their legend.

Grandson Bruce Low retains a few small items, such as a bright red gothic cast iron dragon ashtray, some vases, his grandfather's watch and some pieces Nellie could not bear to part with. But for the most part, the items are gone, reduced to mere debris from Harry Low's notorious days as a high-flying, free-spending rumrunner.

Among the more symbolic of those auctioned items was a pair of white marble lions that once guarded the house's main entryway, reputed to be copies of lions at St. Peter's Basilica at the Vatican. Valued at $1,500 in 1934, and undoubtedly many times more today if they still exist, they were sold for $100.

One of the most valuable of the items was the Lows' dining room suite. The suite was built in the United States specifically to be displayed at the famous Wembley Exhibition. Consisting of a marble-topped buffet, intricately inlaid cabinet, dining table and several upholstered chairs, it was valued at $8,000 and sold for just $525. It was said that just four such sets were ever made. Besides the Lows', one set was, in 1934, to be found in the baronial home of an English peer while two others were owned by U.S. residents.

The Heintzman grand piano was catalogued at $1,800 and sold for $475. A Royal Tabriz Persian rug valued at $2,200 went for $385. A pair of hand-carved Carrara marble vases valued at $1,000 sold for $105. A life-sized Venus de Milo statue bought in Italy and valued at $1,100 brought $90. The carved solid

After losing the house, some of the items Harry and Nellie Low kept include a dragon ashtray, silverware, vases and a watch.

walnut bedroom suite had a stated value of $650 and sold for $280.

A player piano, Chinese rugs, furniture suites, Sheffield tea service, decanters, oil paintings and watercolours. Even an elaborate electric reducing cabinet that elicited laughter when it was placed on offer. Each sold for far less than its value.

Ultimately, the house itself went unsold as bids pushed no higher than $20,000.

When the sale was over and the house sat empty, an eerie quiet settled over it.

The house moves on

After Harry and Nellie Low lost their home and moved to the United States in 1934, Devonshire Lodge passed on to London insurance broker Philip J. Pocock who had held the mortgage they took out on it in 1931. The broker would have preferred to sell the house, but it was in the depths of the Great Depression and there was little interest in the monster home.

The price offered at auction seemed ridiculously low. Harry Low had spent $130,000 to build it and even during the Depression, there were people with money in the Windsor area. Why, then, couldn't the house attract a higher price? Did Windsorites think it was really all that ugly? It was certainly different from the more traditional Tudors and stately Victorians and examples of Arts and Crafts construction that lined Walkerville's quiet streets, but ugly? Just a few years earlier, the local press had hailed it as Harry Low's "beautiful residence" and Canadian Homes and Gardens magazine called it "one of the most impressive in the Border Cities."

Perhaps "Harry's rockpile" frightened away interest for other reasons. Maybe it was the strong association with an era most of Windsor would rather just forget. Maybe, just as Windsor had turned its back on Harry Low and all that he represented, now it was turning its back on his house, too.

By the 1930s, Windsor and the other Border Cities had shaken off their reliance on the wild and lawless days of Prohibition. Windsor's reputation as Canada's Monte Carlo had passed. After the United States legislated an end to Prohibition in 1933, the Border Cities Star declared Windsor "the most law-abiding city in Canada." According to the newspaper, there was no drunkenness, no open sale of beer and liquor and no liquor prosecutions.

The Star's belief that the city should forget those bad old days reflected mainstream public opinion of the era. Many of the businessmen with whom Low had associated had given up the liquor trade and "gone legit". Harry Low's name was not one often repeated in polite Windsor company.

One of the few prospective buyers willing to consider the house was David Croll, who served as Windsor's mayor from 1931 to 1934, when he ran for and won a Windsor seat in the Ontario legislature. Gord Low, nephew of Harry and Nellie, says he was told by his father, Harry's brother, Syd, that Croll was ready to put an offer on the house, saying he wished to use it for a meeting centre for Windsor's Jewish community. The offer was dropped, said Low, because it was made clear to Croll that a Jewish centre "would not be welcome" in Walkerville.

While that incident is not mentioned in James Warren's book about Croll, The People's Senator,

Wembley Exhibition: Officially called the British Empire Exhibition, it was held in Wembley, England in 1924-25 to display items from around the world, its intention to stimulate inter-empire trade.

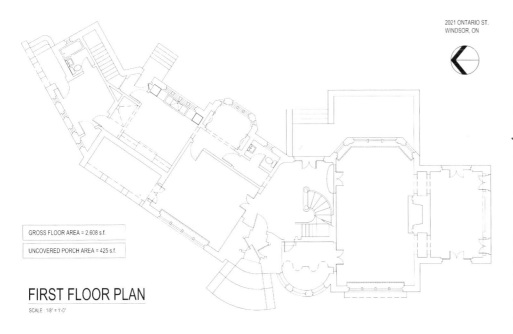

GROSS FLOOR AREA = 2,608 s.f.

UNCOVERED PORCH AREA = 425 s.f.

FIRST FLOOR PLAN
SCALE : 1/8" = 1'-0"

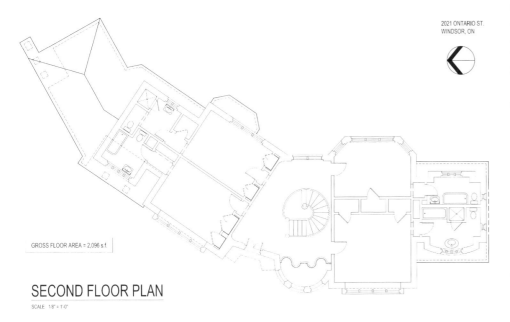

GROSS FLOOR AREA = 2,096 s.f.

SECOND FLOOR PLAN
SCALE : 1/8" = 1'-0"

Architect Jason Grossi produced a floorplan of the house.

the writer does refer to the Walkerville of the era as "a region known for not allowing Jews or blacks to purchase homes."

Still owned by Pocock, the house remained vacant through 1935 and 1936, but the following year, John L. Tessier, manager of a Windsor branch of the Bank of Nova Scotia, rented it from Pocock and his wife. Tessier didn't stay long, however, and in 1938, the Pococks were finally able to sell it.

In October of that year, ownership of Devonshire Lodge passed to Helen P. Wells, wife of Pearson Wells, who served for a time as treasurer for the Dominion Forge and Stamping Company. Dominion Forge was established in 1910 at the request of Henry Ford and the Ford Motor Company of Canada, to provide forgings and stampings. Previously, these products had to be ferried across from Detroit. Dominion Forge produced car parts and diversified into other metal products during the 1930s.

Before coming to Windsor, Helen and Pearson Wells had lived in St. George, New Brunswick. The couple was accustomed to luxurious living accommodation, having owned a beautiful estate home called Dominion Hill, before Pearson accepted the posting at Dominion Forge. Helen Wells paid $28,000 for the house and lived there until her death on October 16, 1948.

While the house sat as part of the estate of Helen Wells, it was temporarily inhabited by Leo Girard, who owned Girard Automotive parts and repair shop on Park Street West. Girard remained in the house only a few months, however, before it was sold for even less money than Mrs. Wells had paid a decade before.

Donald Duff, son of Ruth and Noble Duff who operated Duff Motors in the Royal Windsor Garage downtown, purchased Devonshire Lodge for just $25,000 in June 1949. Donald Duff opened his own dealership on Wyandotte Street East, called Riverside Motors, and later took over his father's operation as well. The house remained in the possession of Duff, and later his company, until 1960 when it was sold to Alice Eleanor Martin, wife of Paul Martin Sr.

Coincidentally, Paul Martin had been Harry Low's lawyer for a time and helped the Lows keep the federal government at bay in 1934 when it tried to seize their furniture and furnishings as payment toward Harry's tax arrears. Coincidentally, too, Mrs. Martin was frequently known as "Nell", just as Norah Low was called "Nellie" by her friends and family.

When the house had come onto the market in 1960, it seemed a good time for the Martins. Paul Martin had served for years as an MP and cabinet minister in the Liberal governments of Mackenzie King and Louis St. Laurent. The turnover of government to the Conservatives in 1957 that put Martin on the opposition benches left him more time to spend in Windsor, until the Liberals were re-elected to government in 1963. Over the coming years, the house served as host to two sitting Liberal prime ministers, Lester Pearson and Pierre Trudeau, during trips they took to Windsor.

In an interview with the writer, former prime minister Paul Martin Jr., son of Paul and Alice Martin, said the house required "a fair amount of renovation when they bought it." The biggest single expense was incurred during the 1960s when the Martins replaced the original cedar roof, by that time

Paul Martin and his son, Paul Martin Jr., in the library of Devonshire Lodge. (Courtesy Paul Martin Jr.)

A view of Devonshire Lodge from 1928, the year Harry Low moved in. (Canadian Homes & Gardens)

leaking, with a less expensive asphalt shingle version that attempted to simulate the rolling style.

In 1992, the asphalt roof was already showing signs of wear and the city contacted the Martins to advise there could be municipal financial help if they were interested in replacing it with the original cedar shingling. It wasn't long before her husband died when Alice Martin contacted the city planning department in response:

> I do hope that it will be years (but I know it is just around the corner) before we have to re-roof our house and home. How nice if we could put on the Country Cottage Roof, but I get goose bumps at the cost. We had Riverside Roofing put a new roof on the coach house. It is stunning; expensive but stunning. (The doggoned "stinky" GST made this little ole lady so annoyed). But … when our roof starts being rambunctious I am putting the papers you sent on file, and I will call.

One feature the house never had was a swimming pool, a fact that reportedly led Paul Martin Sr. to drop in frequently on pool-owning neighbours for a dip. Retired Windsor Star columnist Jim Cornett once fondly recalled Martin "roamed the neighbourhood," sometimes in his bathing suit with a towel around his neck, looking for a place to take a dip.

The Martins lived in the house the rest of their lives. Paul Martin died in 1992 and Alice died the year after. In their latter days in the house, while making estate arrangements, the Martins had offered to donate Devonshire Lodge to the University of Windsor, but the offer was rejected because it was felt maintenance would be too expensive.

Discussions with the city about a prospective heritage designation began in 1993, not long before Alice Martin's death. Her son, Paul Jr., attended a meeting between his mother and city staff. Notes taken of the meeting by then-heritage planner Evelyn McLean reveal Alice Martin's views of the house's rumrunner history and how they differed from those of her son.

"Mrs. Martin does not approve of the reference (to Harry Low)," McLean wrote. "However, Mr. Martin finds that the association with the legendary rumrunner adds to the historical interest, and sees no reason to downplay the fact in the context of the history of the house." Designation was put on hold soon afterwards when Alice Martin died.

Of his mother's opinion, Paul Martin Jr. later told the writer: "My dad used to tell everybody this was Harry Low's house and my mother would say, 'stop telling everyone'."

Martin says while his parents bought the house after he had left home to attend university, he often visited and fell in love with the house. His fondest memory, he says, is of his father sitting in his chair in the library, working on his memoirs, published in two volumes as A Very Public Life.

In 1995, the Martins' estate sold the house for $650,000 to bingo hall owners Wayne Pike and his wife, Sharon Ann Romnycia, and used the proceeds to establish the Nell and Paul Martin Charitable Foundation, a charitable trust.

Urban development expert James Yanchula, in a report to the Windsor Architectural Conservation

Under the ownership of Frank Vella in 2008, Devonshire Lodge's asphalt shingle roof is replaced by a cedar shingle roof more in keeping with the original.

Advisory Committee, said that the house and coach house were in very good condition after the Martins lived there. When they first bought the property, he said, the buildings were in need of basic repairs.

"Having appreciated the architectural value of the house, they immediately undertook repairs and have since continued to maintain it in the spirit of authenticity of design."

But the Martins did very little to change the house and that fact alone could actually have been their greatest contribution to its preservation, says real estate agent Rob Gruich, a long-time admirer of heritage homes, and Devonshire Lodge in particular. "I've seen many grand colonial houses turned into '70s puke," he says.

Windsor heritage committee member and preservation activist Robin Easterbrook concurs. The Martins' sensitivity in preserving the home's past was invaluable, he says. "It would probably be a parking lot if not for Paul Martin."

Pike and Romnycia lived in the house for a few years and said they spent $100,000 in repairs before putting it back on the real estate market for $1.2 million. There were no takers. For a time they also sold antiques from the house.

In 2003, they offered it for sale again, this time for $750,000. In a newspaper interview early the next year, they said since Paul Martin Jr. had become prime minister in December 2003, interest in the place had really picked up. "Everybody wants to see the home," Romnycia said.

But, she admitted, the house was a hard sell. "It takes a certain kind of person to want to live in a home like that," she said. "You wouldn't buy it to renovate it. It does not have all of the toys and whistles that new homes have today."

Finally, with the house sitting on the market and unsold for the better part of a decade, the couple applied to the city for approval to subdivide the property, so they could offer the coach house/garage in a separate listing.

"No one today is building a home with separate servant's quarters," real estate agent Doug Jeffrey explained at the time. At more than 1,400 square feet, he said, the coach house could well stand as a separate property.

The city denied the application, a decision that was later upheld by the Ontario Municipal Board.

Then, rumors swirled that the owners intended to demolish the house. Nothing could be further

A closeup of how cedar shingles are laid to replicate thatching. (Fine Homebuilding magazine)

from the truth, assured Jeffrey. The property is just too big to sell as-is.

Devonshire Lodge received official historical designation from the city in 2007 and finally, in April 2008, Frank Vella, owner of Walkerville Pharmacy, bought the house for $460,000. Vella said at the time he planned to sink $500,000 into renovations.

Vella grew up in Windsor's neighbouring "Little Italy" community around Erie Street, and admired the house for years before he bought it at the age of 29. "I look at that house not as a structure, but as an

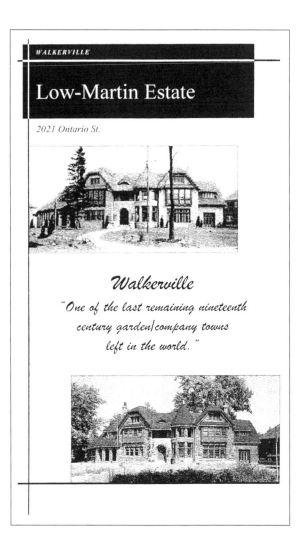

Low-Martin Estate

2021 Ontario St.

Walkerville

"One of the last remaining nineteenth century garden/company towns left in the world."

Harry Low

The Low-Martin house was built in 1928 for Harry Low, a toolmaker who became one of the giants of the rum-running trade during Prohibition. The house was originally called "Devonshire Lodge" and these words are embedded in the front walkway. Harry Low spared no expense in the construction of his mansion which cost him nearly $130,000 to build. The Depression and legal problems lost Low his house on Ontario Street in the early 1930s. Low died in Windsor in 1955.

Death Takes Harry Low, 67
Liquor King Saw Empire Fall in Ruin
Windsor Star

Windsor, Aug. 23, 1955— Harry Low, one of the most colourful figures of a colourful era in the history of Windsor, died Sunday at Hotel Dieu after a short illness. He was 65 and had been living for some time at 272 McKay.

Born in Ottawa, Mr. Low came to Windsor as a young man and worked in Detroit, where he was considered a top toolmaker. However, when the famous 18th Amendment to the U.S. constitution was passed and the Volstead Act came into being, Mr. Low saw his chance to get into a lucrative profession.

Operating from a Detroit River dock, Mr. Low and his associates waybilled liquor in fast speedboats ostensibly headed for Cuba or the West Indies. Actually, the liquor went directly across the river for sale in Detroit.

By the time the Roaring Twenties were drawing to a close, Mr. Low was reputed to have several million dollars and his home in Walkerville was, and still is, one of the showplaces of a town that was renowned for fine homes.

The Martins

In 1961 renowned Canadian politician Paul Martin Sr. and his wife Nell bought the house for a mere $22,000. Paul Martin has been referred to as "Windsor's most famous son" and has made his mark in local and Canadian history – representing Windsor from 1935 to 1968, serving as High Commissioner to Great Britain in the 1970s, and helping establish many of Canada's social programs. It is well known that 2021 Ontario St. became a meeting place for great politicians such as Lester Pearson and Pierre Trudeau, and it is in the basement study of this home that that he wrote his memoirs.

Paul Martin Jr. followed his father's footsteps into politics, serving as Canada's Finance Minister before becoming Prime Minister on December 8, 2003.

Well–known Landmark
Windsor Star
Marty Gervais

"Everybody in the city knows the place, and you could never duplicate it."

The memory of the house still tugs at the heart of Federal Finance Minister Paul Martin whose teenage years were spent there. That's why he drove by it last week when he was in town.

"I went by it, and you know, the only thing missing is a sign for Shaughnessy Cohen," says the ever political younger Martin.

"My mother's probably pretty steamed about this in heaven right now wondering where it is."

Martin's memory of his mother Nell, and his elder statesman father, revolve around a small plain-looking room off the kitchen.

"That's where they lived," he told me on the phone from his LaSalle-Emard riding office.

"That back room is the size of a clothes closet…. It had no particular decoration…. That's where my parents lived. They'd sit back there and watch TV.

"I always said to them, 'You don't need a big house—you need a clothes closet.'"

Paul Martin Sr. died in 1992, and Nell Martin in 1993.

Real estate pamphlet describes the house. (Courtesy Rob Gruich)

organism," he says. "It breathes. There's a fluidity to the architecture."

His plan was to restore and live in the house. "It was a challenge I could sink my teeth into." His real estate agent, Rob Gruich, "thought I was crazy. I said I don't care what you think, just get me that house."

His first walk through the house brought into stark reality just what a huge job he had taken on and much of the work was going to be things that no one would ever see: fixing sewer lines, removing mould and asbestos. During cleanup, he filled seven or eight giant construction bins with demolition deb-

ris. There were sewage backups and flooding during storms.

With the help of city heritage funds, Vella replaced the old asphalt shingle roof the Martins had installed, a job that cost more than $150,000. The city paid about one-third.

Vella quickly came to realize that in a very real sense, the house belonged to the community. "It comes with a certain notoriety and lack of privacy. Deep in my heart, I always felt the house did not belong to me, because it was such an important place. The house has a power that is almost mysterious."

When he reluctantly put the house on the market, he was glad that Vern Myslichuk was the one to buy it. "Vern shared my enthusiasm for the house. I knew he was going to do it justice."

City heritage planner John Calhoun credits Vella with "stabilizing" the property. "It had been let go pretty badly," he says. Vella "did the major task of doing what had to be done to protect the house from the elements, such as putting on a new roof. His job was as stabilizer. What might have happened? The fear was that it would continue to have water infiltration and gradually ruin all of the interior. The stone walls would have largely stayed intact, but the interior would have been lost. Plaster would have dissolved, the wood would have gotten mouldy.

"Its uniqueness would have remained its shape, but not what it would have been," says Calhoun.

He says that when Vern Myslichuk took over, "structurally, the house was fine. Except for the basement beneath the back porch, it seemed plumb and the floors looked flat to me."

Realtor Rob Gruich puts it this way: "Frank Vella saved the house from the wrecking ball. Vern Myslichuk took it from there."

Vern Myslichuk bought Devonshire Lodge in April 2012. Now it was time to get down to business.

BetterMade Cabinets owner Vern Myslichuk bought Devonshire Lodge in April 2012. (Windsor Star)

Chapter 7:

Vern Myslichuk's Restoration

HARRY LOW, THE MAN WHO conceived of and built Devonshire Lodge, came to Windsor in search of a better, more prosperous life for himself and his family. The man who bought the house in 2012, 84 years after it had been completed, has an instinctive empathy for Low's entrepreneurial zeal. In fact, as Vern Myslichuk learned more about Low, he started to develop a sense of kinship with the man.

Myslichuk can imagine Low standing boldly on the empty plot of land at Devonshire Road and Ontario Street, the place where he would build his monster of a home, and gazing across the road at James Cooper's hulking mansion, Cooper Court. "I have this vision of Harry next to (builder) George Lawton and raising his arms and saying, 'let's build it right here.' And that's just what they did."

Harry Low's no-nonsense approach to business drove him to be always on the lookout for "the next big thing," says Myslichuk. It is a spirit that drives Myslichuk himself.

Vern Myslichuk arrived in Windsor from Western Canada in 1984, a young man in search of a job. He found employment in an automotive stamping plant and while he hated every day of it, a steady progression of pay raises kept him a slave to the company for 14 years. Through those years, however, he was always dabbling at other things on the side, always determined to find a way to create a better life for himself.

Like Harry Low, Myslichuk was skilled with his hands. Low had been a master tool and die maker; Myslichuk had a knack for building things from wood. In the early years he built decks and occasionally took on other woodworking projects. One day he took a stab at cabinetry and produced his own kitchen.

Myslichuk was eager to learn and to put his skills to better use. He began visiting the public library and looking up books about cabinetry and how to start a business. Luckily, the library was a place that could also accommodate his young daughter, Corey. He brought her along and while she occupied herself playing with toys, he sat by her side and spent his time reading everything he could get his hands on.

From what he learned there, Myslichuk opened a business in his garage and started refinishing furniture. He would go to garage sales, pick up worn pieces of furniture for a couple of dollars, refinish them and sell them for 20, 30, maybe $50.

One day someone asked him if he did kitchens and he told them no, that wasn't the business he was in. He woke up in the early hours of the next morning and sat straight up in bed. "Wait a minute," he said to himself. "What was I thinking? Why not do kitchens?"

"I got up that day and registered the name, BetterMade Cabinets and it completely changed my whole way of thinking. I rewrote my business plan. I called up my old clients and told them, 'I'm doing kitchens now.'"

But that wasn't all. He began buying properties and fitting them out with fine cabinetry, confident that a stunning kitchen would attract eager buyers. He was right.

Myslichuk had never heard of Harry Low before he came to Windsor – nor of his house. After moving to the city, he would occasionally hear people speak of the old Harry Low house, but it was not until 15 years after he first arrived that he finally set eyes on it. It happened one day when by chance, he found himself driving past the corner of Ontario Street and Devonshire Road.

"I looked up and said, 'Whoa. That must be the house people are talking about.' The house kind of just went, 'boom, look at me'."

Afterwards, he would frequently drive through the neighbourhood so that he could stop outside to study the house. "I'd sit out there in my car, right at the corner. I was like a house-stalker," he jokes. He loved the unusual wavy roof and the stone, and later incorporated aspects of the exterior design into his own homes.

While it was love at first sight, it would take another dozen years before Myslichuk was able to acquire the house. He missed his first chance: When the house came onto the market in 2007, Myslichuk was preoccupied with building his kitchen cabinet business, and wasn't in any position to swing a deal for the crumbling mansion. Then, when Frank Vella bought it the next year, Myslichuk felt "Well, that's that. He'll likely own the place forever. I started to put the thought of ever owning it out of my mind."

Yet his fascination with the house continued. Even if he couldn't own it, he was determined to play a part in bringing the house back to its magnificence. "Even at that moment, I thought I want to do the kitchen for the new owner. I thought, I'll do it for free. I just wanted to be part of that house."

But as chance would have it, Vella discovered four years later that he himself faced an important choice: His pharmacy business was expanding quickly and required his fulltime attention. If he was going to devote that attention to business, he didn't have the time and energy to devote to the restoration of Devonshire Lodge. And so he reluctantly placed it back on the market.

This time, Myslichuk says, "I wasn't going to let it get away. I was going to find a way to have it." Little did he know at the time what a rocky road it would be to ultimate ownership. No one wanted to finance the deal. Lenders would take one look at the place and tell him, "not a chance." Getting it appraised was another struggle because there was no other house anywhere in the region with which to compare it.

Original Address: Devonshire Lodge's address today is 2021 Ontario Street. Originally, before Walkerville became part of Windsor in 1935, the address was 288 Devonshire Road, Walkerville, Ontario.

Harry Low's audacious dream restored.

Vern Myslichuk holds a news conference in June 2012 to announce his plans for the restoration.

the excitement among his employees was palpable. "Some of them had been part of the renovation with the previous owner but now we were going to be it. The excitement and the shock were just overwhelming. Everybody wanted to be out here. Everybody wanted to be part of it, to help. They kept asking, 'What can I do?'"

Telephone calls poured in from the news media, but Myslichuk insisted there would be no interviews until he was ready. He wanted to hold a news conference on the front lawn, prepared a speech and had one door refinished so that it could be displayed next to an unfinished one to give everyone an idea about what was about to happen to the entire house.

The day of the media event, "I was giddy. I was like a kid with a new toy. I practised my speech for two hours. Then I threw it away. I was so excited. I ended up just talking."

It began to rain so the press conference had to be brought inside. As people passed by, they wondered what the commotion was and began arriving at the front door. Before he knew it, an impromptu tour had been organized and Myslichuk was showing neighbours around the grand old home. The experience gave him an idea: Why not hold occasional viewings to let members of the public witness his progress? Why not let them see for themselves how he was going to bring this "shame of Walkerville" back to its glorious past?

And so over the next two years of reconstruction, tours were held, with entry fee revenue donated to charity. It was the commencement of a beautiful relationship between the community and Devonshire Lodge.

Finally, the call came from one lender in April 2012. The house could be his. But the drama never stopped. "From there, I couldn't find anyone to insure it. Sometimes I just got tired of making calls and asked myself whether this was just a crazy idea. But I got my second wind and I said, 'You know what? I'll keep calling people until someone says yes.'" Finally, he found an insurer.

Back at his shop on Odessa Drive, Myslichuk says

Monster of a mess

Vern Myslichuk had been through the house several times before he actually bought it, estimating the cost of the work that needed to be done. But on the first day that he owned it, he took a long walk through the house, pausing to study details of its condition. "I literally cried. It was not what I thought it was going to be."

The stone structure was solid, but the wood and plaster details were a wreck.

"I had this image of grandeur in my mind and it was far from grand. It was pathetic. It was so horrible. There were holes in the floor and the ceiling. Everything was damaged. There was nothing left to love. It was a beautiful home on the outside but inside, it was sad. I was emotionally a mess. I went home thinking, do I really want that? Then I took 20 minutes and I pulled myself together and I came back at it."

The holding of the press conference, and that impromptu tour marked the start, Myslichuk thinks, of people believing it might just happen. Devonshire Lodge might be saved yet. Many had feared this day would never come and that the house would rot away from neglect, or else be torn down.

Myslichuk drew up a work plan that entailed not just renovating the house, but of restoring it to reflect the period in which it was built. There would be modern conveniences and technology, of course, but the underlying theme would be that of the 1920s. When he was finished, Myslichuk wanted the house to present itself in all of its Flapper-era splendour, with all of its eccentricities intact.

He decided he would start on the outside of the house. He wanted people to see for themselves that

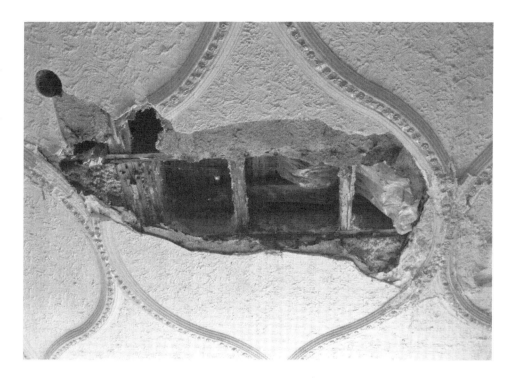

Holes in the ceiling required extensive plaster restoration.

progress was being made. His daughter, Corey, and son, Eric, were eager to help. Staff from BetterMade Cabinets could hardly wait to get at it. That first weekend before doing anything to the house, however, they cut the lawn, trimmed the shrubs and generally got the grounds in shape.

Then throughout the summer of 2012, Myslichuk and his workers spent their time scraping, sanding, repairing big holes in the window frames, sashes and sills, and otherwise making the house look lived-in again. He decided there would be no sandblasting of the stone because he feared that would ruin its integrity. As they worked, passersby would stop to offer encouragement.

"It seemed like every car was stopping and people were hopping out and coming up to me and talking. They'd ask me about the place and congratulate me and wish us the best of luck. And sometimes you got the idea they were saying 'good luck' (in an ironic way). You could hear them saying to themselves, 'Sure, sure. You'll be selling it, just like the other guy.' I think everybody was saying to one another it's not going to happen. You could see it in their eyes and their expressions. They were encouraging, but you could see they were saying to themselves, 'You might as well call it quits now'."

But Myslichuk was determined to succeed. He gathered quotes on work that needed to be done to the interior, quotes that sometimes sent him reeling. After he budgeted $27,000 for one project, a quote came in for $100,000. "I thought, it was going to be spectacular at 27 (thousand), so how could it be at a hundred (thousand)?"

As a businessman himself, Myslichuk understood that a tradesman's quote must anticipate and build in the uncertainties. Whether it's electrical, plumbing or heating, a businessman has to be ready for every eventuality, for everything that remains hidden behind the walls – even when those walls are crumbling. For example, "The heating guys came in and they had to put ductwork in a house that wasn't designed for ductwork." And so the costs mounted.

So did the excitement.

"Everyone was so fired up. I'd be here with people working inside at 6, 7 o'clock in the morning. I never had to ask anyone to come in or stay late. They just did it."

The workers' pride was evident from the begin-ning. One tradesman told Myslichuk he wanted to produce a family Christmas card and he wanted to use the house as a backdrop. He wondered if that would be okay. "So I said of course, and he had a photo taken of him and his wife with the house. He was just so happy and proud of the house that he'd worked on."

By the time half of the exterior of the house was finished, the contrast was stunning. "You could compare and see the progress," says Myslichuk. "People would stop and compliment us. It was a real encouragement to the workers."

One of the biggest surprises came while they were stripping and repairing the second-floor windows on the front of the house. "We were changing the mouldings because they were so rotted. We started taking the mouldings off and all of a sudden someone realized, hey, wait a minute, these panels aren't wood. They're stamped copper."

The panels were carefully removed and lowered to the ground. Myslichuk used various cleaners to work his way down through the paint layers that had been applied over the decades and, after a lot of hard work, the beautiful gleaming copper panels were revealed once more.

"It was the worst job ever," says Myslichuk. "I was cleaning these things and I was beside myself at the same time. I was like a kid, I was so excited. One of those big 'eureka' moments."

Even long-time neighbours of the old house were astonished at the discovery. No one had ever guessed that the panels were anything but wood. Over time, these gleaming copper panels, along with the copper eavestroughs, will form a rich, pale green patina, just

Covered with layers of paint, the panels beneath the front windows are revealed as stamped copper.

Vern Myslichuk discovered the fireplace poker set buried in basement rubble.

like the roofs of the Parliament Buildings.

One day soon after Myslichuk had purchased the house, a man drove up and introduced himself to the new owner as Bruce Low, grandson of Harry Low. Low and Myslichuk struck up a bond based on their mutual fascination with, and respect for, Harry Low. They met frequently afterward, with Low showing up one time with a number of old photographs from his grandfather's era. "He was so happy to see the house being brought back to life," says Myslichuk.

Everything took more effort than he expected. But in exchange for that effort, there were happy surprises, such as the discovery of the original fireplace poker set amidst debris in the basement. "It was there for years and nobody had been looking for it. It was one of those moments that I grabbed it and held it and I was afraid somebody was going to take it out of my hands. I was so excited."

His proudest moment, he says, was when the exterior of the house was finished, even before the inside work was really begun. "The moment I could stand at the road and say, 'Yes! Now it's a house again!' For the people of the neighbourhood, for me, it was very satisfying. It had been such an eyesore for so many years."

The Windows

There are nearly 100 wood frame windows in Devonshire Lodge, windows that had been built to last. Vern Myslichuk decided early on that while it would definitely be easier to replace the windows than to repair them, "That wasn't going to happen. We would do whatever we had to, to restore the originals."

At first, Myslichuk and his restoration crew thought it would be a simple task to remove the windows, repair them and put them back in place. And for the hinged windows at least, that was the approach that was taken. For the sash windows that were designed to slide up and down in a track, however, it was a very different matter.

"These windows were built with no thought of ever having to take them apart," says Myslichuk. "Today, it takes five minutes to take a door or a window apart. Here, every piece was interlocked with the next piece so you couldn't just take one piece out to get to the one behind it. To take one piece apart, you had to break it to get to the next piece."

The windows that were hinge-hung were easily removed, taken to the shop, sanded, primed and painted. "Once the window was out, we just sanded it down with air compressors, put it into a spray booth, then reglazed, repainted and brought the window back and put it back into a structure we had just rebuilt."

The sash windows where the frames slid in tracks were a different matter, and most of the windows were of that type. At one time, they considered tearing apart all the frames and building new ones, then reinstalling the old windows. It proved to be not quite that simple. The windows were rotted, the frames, sills and jambs pocked with holes, some large enough to allow rodents to enter the house.

"We experimented, trying to figure out what was going to work. I'd strip down a window and sand it, use marine epoxies to fix the holes in the wood, then actually reshape the wood. I sanded it 80 per cent of the way, reglazed, put the window back togeth-er. Sometimes the holes were so big there was more epoxy than wood. And when it was finished, it looked like a horrible job.

"We realized we had to sand right back to the bare wood. You couldn't leave any paint residue. Every flake of paint had to come off."

So how best to get down to the bare wood? And quickly? "We tried sanding wheels and scrapers. We did heat guns, strippers, soda blasting. The soda blaster blew the old wood apart. The only way we were able to get it down to the wood is by using some strippers and hand scraping. Right down to the bare wood."

It was a process that was repeated for each one of the windows. "As we moved forward, we improved," says Myslichuk. "We got a system down. You start to get in the groove, to feel it. It's simple, it's just a lot of grunt work."

Holes in the sills, trims and mouldings were sometimes gaping and over the years, any material at hand, including chicken wire, had been stuffed into the holes. In such cases, epoxy and filler were inadequate. "We would cut out pieces of new wood, scribe the piece of wood, sand it down to the shape of the moulding and replace it."

As they removed the windows, the workmen discovered small circular metal tags that had been pressed into the wood frame of each window, with a number stamped onto each one. Evidently this was the identification system. As the windows were produced off-site, the numbers made it easy to determine where each one was to go when it was delivered to the house. Each window was custom built especially for its unique location.

Neglected for years, the rotten windows had to be repaired and sanded down. Not a speck of paint was left before they were primed and repainted.

Vern Myslichuk's daughter, Corey, works on the windows.

When the house was constructed, each of the nearly 100 windows was tagged so it could be installed in the location for which it was custom built.

The unusual curved windows in the rounded turret portion at the front of the house were repaired in place because Myslichuk feared they would shatter if they were taken out. All of the windows were retained as single-pane because that's the way they originally were, says Myslichuk. To maintain the original look, no storm windows were added.

Plasterwork

Andrew Ledoux's family has been creating and restoring plaster for about three centuries. It all began back in France and the family brought their skills with them to the New World when they immigrated to Quebec in the 1730s. Their descendants continue the practice to this day in Windsor and Detroit under the name Ledoux Interiors.

Vern Myslichuk knew exactly whom to call upon when he saw the condition of his ceilings. "I look at what they did and shake my head," he says. "It was amazing. How they could blend something new into something that's 80 years old, and you'd never know they did it."

"It was daunting," says Andrew Ledoux about the huge project. "Just looking at the scope of what had to be done." But, adds the man who began to learn his trade at the age of 10, "We've been doing the same work in my family for generations. I was excited at the prospect of having to restore it properly. I pride myself in being able to handle any problem. This was one of the most complicated I've encountered. This house is out of the ordinary."

He says the original work was clearly achieved by highly skilled tradesmen. A good restorer can see and understand everything that was originally there, he says. For instance, he describes the fibreboard that was installed beneath the ceiling plaster as state-of-the-art for its time. However, he adds, it is a product that wasn't used for a long period because it didn't stand up. And that, he says, is part of the reason there was so much damage to the ceilings.

Ledoux says he has seen the same plaster crown moulding design before, although never to the extent it was used at Devonshire Lodge. "It was a classical crown moulding design that was popular in the early 1900s. Very popular in Detroit."

He was particularly drawn to the tracery ceilings because each room's ceiling was done in a different pattern. That would be very expensive to re-create today, he says. He says there are probably 15 or so different moulding details in the plasterwork. Restoration was "fun and unusual," he says. "We used all kinds of different techniques."

Ledoux's father, Gerry, who is "in his 70s," says Ledoux, was delighted to help work on the house. Myslichuk recalls watching Gerry Ledoux hop around on the scaffolding like a man half his age, leaving the owner sometimes breathless in fear that the craftsman would fall. But the surefooted older man did a fabulous job of "feathering in" his modern work with the 1920s details he was charged with replicating, says Myslichuk.

The work done by the Ledoux team also included repairing a large crack in the limestone fireplace and bringing it back to its glory days where it can once more radiate its warmth out into the living room. Sitting to one side of the fireplace is the vintage poker set Myslichuk discovered buried in debris in the basement – placed back in its original spot.

Faced with crumbling ceilings and broken ceiling tracery patterns, master craftsmen Andrew and Gerry Ledoux repaired holes in the ceiling, produced mouldings and feathered in their modern work to make it indistinguishable from that which remained of the original 1928 plasterwork.

Intricate ceiling mouldings, tracery patterns and insert details were repaired throughout the house.

Doors

The doors of Devonshire Lodge are constructed from a variety of woods. The front entrance door is white oak, as are the vestibule and the panelling in the front closet. Yet once inside the grand two-storey entrance hall, walnut takes over.

Windsor architect Jason Grossi explains the probable logic of that plan. He says in most mansions of the early 1900s, white oak was used because the closed-cell grain structure of the old-growth wood made it suitable for areas of the house exposed to the elements.

Today, the more common and less weather-resistant red oak is much more prevalent in homes because it is faster growing and therefore relatively cheaper and more obtainable than white oak.

Grossi says traditionally, different types of wood were used to differentiate rooms or areas of grand homes, to create themes. "Walnut sometimes for dining and cherry for living rooms, for example. In the early 1900s people knew their wood species right away and knew what craftsmanship was," he says.

Myslichuk says some of the outer doors at the back of the house were mysteriously constructed of an inexpensive and unidentifiable wood on the outside, then trimmed on the inside with a more expensive one-eighth-inch walnut veneer. The paintable exterior was coated in about 10 layers.

To restore the home's main entranceway, the front door was removed and taken to the shop for repair. The frame was repaired on site. The door was restained to match portions of the old trim Myslichuk believes represents the original shade of the door.

One other discovery that impressed Myslichuk

An example of the door trim that was scribed to the stonework.

was the "scribing" of the door trim to the exterior stonework. "The stone is rough and it must have taken forever. Today, it's normal to put the trim on first and put the stone against the trim. To do it this way is much harder. The skill level was amazing."

The exterior library doors were removed, taken to the BetterMade Cabinets shop for repair and sanding, and then repainted.

Cabinetry and woodwork

When Vern Myslichuk decided to buy Devonshire Lodge, he reasoned that most of the restoration work involved wood. And after all, he owned Better-Made Cabinets, a company that produces kitchen cabinets, wall units, buffets, hutches and entertainment centres. "Wood is what we do," he says. "We were ideally suited to this job."

And while he might have not yet understood the extent of all the other work that was required to get the house back into shape, a great deal of the effort went toward replacing and restoring the wood. Besides the restoring of windows, doors and floors, however, Myslichuk set to work creating new panelling and cabinetry throughout the house, in a style that would do justice to the home's grandeur.

He wanted the key areas of the house to convey a "stately 1920s masculine" vibe, and based the concept upon a photograph of another house from that era sent to him by a friend. This theme is evident especially in the master bedroom and the living room.

He opened up the master bedroom ceiling, creating the space for a new barrel-panelled ceiling that soars above the custom-made bed. Around the perimeter of the upper reaches of the newly opened space he built large display cabinets. Medallions and carved lion's heads on the bedposts were worked into the woodwork to add further to the room's gravitas.

"When we installed the bed in that room, it just belonged there," he says. "It was a perfect fit with the heaviness of the ceiling and the shelving and panelling."

The masculine feel of the house is subtly softened somewhat by a recurring theme of a floret that can

The master bedroom ceiling was opened up and barrel panels installed. Custom cherry wood panelling and cabinetry were created in the BetterMade Cabinets shop, finished a rich dark colour and installed. The custom bed (previous page) was a natural fit with the finished room. A doorway was created to an adjoining bedroom which was turned into a dressing room.

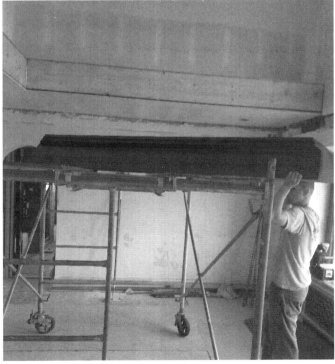

Custom cherry wood panelling and cabinetry were created in the BetterMade Cabinets shop.

be found in the stone and plasterwork. The lion's head is repeated in the kitchen cabinetry.

The smaller bedroom next to the master was converted into a cabinetry-filled dressing room, with the passage between the two created in such a way it looks as though it was always there.

In the kitchen, Myslichuk was determined to save and repurpose the original icebox that dominated one wall. He had it hauled to his workshop and the back was cut out so the original icebox could be used for storage. This he surrounded with the same dark cherry wood cabinetry used in the dining room and other parts of the house. He kept the original over-sized country sink and added a huge island in the centre of the floor.

"I wanted to restore and repair, but also to make it up to date," he says. "I added cherry wood because that's the popular wood of the day. But I wanted to make it look like it had always been here."

Most of the home's floors are the original oak, some strip and some parquet. Myslichuk kept the parquet once he learned it was original to the house, the pieces nailed down individually. It is another piece of master craftsmanship that sets the house apart.

The kitchen flooring is a softer wood, but since it has withstood the more than eight decades of wear, he knows it's more durable than pine, although in some spots the wood was so thin there was nothing left to sand.

The grand staircase that dominates the central foyer needed repairs – it was damaged by vandals a few years ago – but remains much the way it original-ly looked in 1928.

One of the defining moments during renova-

Heavy equipment is brought in to reach the upper portions of the house.

The parquet floors are found to be original and painstakingly constructed, piece by piece. A sign of the house's sorry state is that a temporary furnace had been installed to limit further damage. The exhaust was piped through a door.

tion came when a group came through the house on a tour and at the end, as they gathered at the base of the staircase, one of the tour members handed Myslichuk a photocopy of a picture. It was a picture of the very staircase where they stood, but taken during construction in 1927.

"There were two gentlemen standing to the side. You could see the stairs were being assembled. There was no ceiling, just rafters. I literally cried. It was so incredible. The lady who gave me the photo, her grandfather had owned Walker Lumber and he had been part of the build of this house."

(The original photograph, found in the files of the former Walker Lumber, is reproduced earlier in this book.)

Heating and cooling

When Myslichuk took possession of the house, he found a temporary furnace in the foyer that had been installed to help control the temperature and prevent further indoor damage from cold and humidity. The furnace was ducted out the door. "It actually looked quite comical to see this furnace in the front room, with the pipe going out the door," he says.

In order for further work to be done over the winter, however, a proper heating system had to be installed. But first, old pipes from the original boiler system had to be removed. "The pipes reminded me of a steamship – everything was so large, so out of proportion. Nothing was ordinary and everything was an obstacle. So we started cutting out the old pipes.

"To run ductwork, you had to bust through block walls. No one complained about the work. They knew it wasn't going to be a typical house when they took the job on. Normally you don't have to remove tonnes of metal before you start laying your ductwork."

Then before the new ducts and two furnaces were installed, insulation was blown in on the inside of the exterior walls. And while the old radiators were no longer a working part of the heating system, Myslichuk retained them for their esthetic appeal.

Despite the lack of double-glazed windows, the size of the home and high ceilings, Myslichuk says the heating system keeps the place cozy and those sturdy stone walls help the air conditioning system keep it comfortable in the summer heat.

Plumbing

The kitchen and library ceilings had been destroyed by torrents of water from pipes that had burst in recent years as the house sat unused and unheated. The hole in the library roof was so large and extensive, you could look through it and see the bottom of the bathtub from the second-storey bathroom. Clearly, it was unsafe and required immediate attention.

Myslichuk called in a plumber to hook up a limited water supply so at least they could get one of the home's seven bathrooms functioning and draw a bucket of water when it was needed. He recalls the day they first turned the water back on.

"Water went shooting out everywhere. What a mess."

The seven bathrooms – four on the second floor, two on the main floor and one in the basement bar – had been originally finished in different colours of tile. Myslichuk had hoped to retain much of the ori-

Modern Bathrooms: The four second-storey bedrooms were each fitted with an ensuite bathroom, each one finished in a different colour of tile. Two of the bathrooms contained body showers, proving that this popular modern-era high-end feature has been around a long time

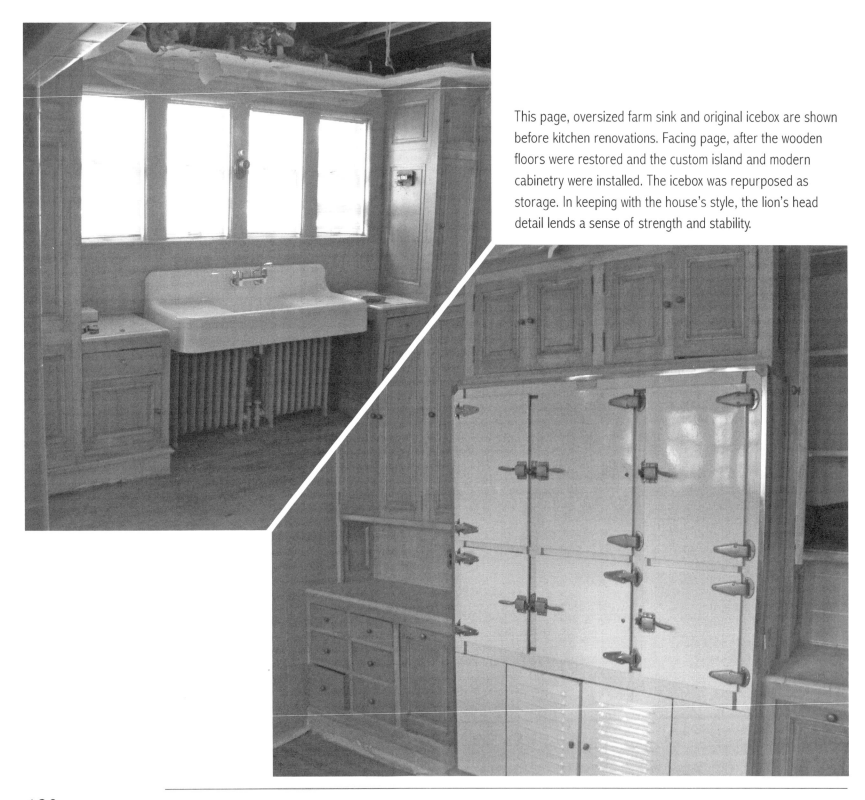

This page, oversized farm sink and original icebox are shown before kitchen renovations. Facing page, after the wooden floors were restored and the custom island and modern cabinetry were installed. The icebox was repurposed as storage. In keeping with the house's style, the lion's head detail lends a sense of strength and stability.

Before repairs to the library ceiling, an upper-floor bathtub hangs through. Afterwards, cherry wood panelling puts the finishing touch to the repairs. The chandelier is original.

ginal bathroom tile, but when repairs began on the plumbing, much of it had to be ripped out. He tried to replace it with similar designs. The master bathroom tile, however, is original.

Foundation work

The portion of the cellar that held Harry Low's bar was caving in. As work commenced on the stone patio that sat above the bar, it was realized that entire portions of the cellar wall needed to be rebuilt. "It was bowing out," says Myslichuk. Surface stones were removed, cleaned, labelled, photographed and piled on wooden skids in the backyard.

"We brought in the front loader and took the wall apart, put in the footings and rebuilt it. The neighbours thought I'd absolutely lost my mind. We ended up with this big hole in the ground. We built the walls bigger, fatter, thicker. But we couldn't go beyond the original footprint because we only had so much stone. We put the stone back exactly the way it was before. Now it looks as though it's always been there."

Electrical

Myslichuk was surprised to discover the original electrical system included a breaker system and says he was told by electricians it was very advanced for its era. There was even a buzzer system to summon staff to key parts of the property: dining room, master bedroom, living room and outdoors. When one of the buttons was pressed, a buzzer would ring in the kitchen. The dining room buzzer sat in the centre of the dining table, the wiring running beneath the table to the centre of the floor.

The wiring was BX armoured cable but there

Harry Low displayed his house address on the back of a board from a box of Pommery & Greno champagne.

were no grounded circuits at the time. The home's wiring was definitely old, says electrician Haitham Rasho of Future Electric, who worked to upgrade the system. He estimates 70 per cent of the wiring was original. "I was surprised it was still working," he says. However, the old wires were brittle with age. With no grounded circuits, there was no breaker to trip, adding to the danger of an electrical fire.

Harry Low's champagne tastes

The numbers of the street address hung on a simple board and by the time Myslichuk purchased the house, one of the numbers had fallen crooked, hanging as a comical statement on the house's general state of disrepair. Myslichuk tossed the board and the numbers into the back of his truck and forgot about them for several weeks. One day he picked them up and for the first time, turned the board over. Carved on it were the words: "Champagne. Pommery & Greno. Reims."

The cellar wall beneath the back porch was crumbling. Face stones were removed and numbered and the foundation wall was removed with a backhoe. The wall was rebuilt on the same footprint, the porch re-poured and the face stones replaced in sequence.

Myslichuk checked out the inscription on the Internet and discovered the history of the Pommery & Greno champagne company in Reims, France. When it was discovered during the research for this book that Harry Low had travelled to Europe, including France, twice – in 1923 and 1927 – a picture began to emerge in his mind.

The plaque is part of a champagne box. "They must have had a box of champagne and I can envision Harry Low standing here and saying, 'That'll work. Put the numbers on the back of that.' We refinished it and put it back up."

A job well done

The moment he set eyes on Harry Low's house, Windsor city heritage planner John Calhoun says, "I knew this was a house that needed to be kept. Its loss would have been a terrible loss to the community. This is quite a magical house."

Had the restoration not been done when it was, says Calhoun, "it could have been lost simply through deteriorization."

Architect and restoration expert Jason Grossi likes what he sees of the restoration work. "There have been no shortcuts here," he says. "The work, the windows, restoration of the frames, is exactly what needed to happen. The new owner is obviously a detail guy. He's done what was necessary to save this house."

It had been Myslichuk's goal to save, restore and preserve Devonshire Lodge for future generations. "This house belongs to the community, too," he says. "I'm living here now, but I understand how important it is to save it for the benefit of the city, for all those people who feel as though they have a stake in it."

Moved in

The move-in date was long delayed, thanks to the inevitable complications of such an immense restoration. Finally, Myslichuk and his daughter, Corey, moved in to Devonshire Lodge in June 2014. Incredibly, given the condition of the house before work began, there had been surprisingly few critters in the building. For a while there had been a bird flying around. Myslichuk is convinced the same bird actually returned after it had been escorted outside. There were signs of a few mice in the attic, but no major infestation of raccoons or squirrels.

In the days after they moved in, Corey told her father she thought she heard what could be mice after she went to bed. Myslichuk himself heard nothing until about a month later.

"I was lying in bed. Everything is silent and I start to hear this rustling. This noise is crazy. It's like a hundred mice. I swear it sounded like they were going to pick up the bed. I could hardly sleep. It was so loud, it was everywhere."

The exterminators were called but were unable to come for a few days so in the interim, he set several traps. "And we caught one mouse," he says. "Just one. And the noise was gone and it never came back."

Sometimes he looks out over the yard and imagines he can see Harry Low himself, contemplating the scene. "This house is crazy. It's insane," says Myslichuk. "But it's Harry Low's vision. And it's been my job to bring it back to life. I think Harry would be pleased.

The fireplace, made of Caen limestone imported from France, had been painted blue.

Weeks of painstaking soda blasting and sanding brought the fireplace back to its magnificence.

A built-in verandah on the back porch from Paul Martin Sr.'s era was removed, leaving a portion of the outside wall painted white. Soda blasting brought it back to its original finish.

"The work we've done has enhanced the house. In fact, sometimes I jokingly said, 'If Harry had had more money, he'd have done it this way.' There was nothing in this house of a poor quality. The kitchen was what it was for the time, but it wasn't over the top, compared to the rest of the house. What I've done suits the house. It's over the top. Just like the house.

"When people look at a lot of the work I've done, they think it's original. We've blended it with the work that was already here, but it was better made. That's what I've always tried to achieve. When I called my company BetterMade, I meant it."

'Now what?'

"Harry did everything to the max," says Myslichuk. "He always went all out. I think my life has been that way too. I'm never satisfied."

Myslichuk studies a photograph of one of Low's two ships, the Vedas, taken as it lay docked along the Windsor waterfront. The image shows people standing alongside the vessel and Myslichuk says it makes him realize how gigantic the craft really was. "It wasn't a boat, it was a ship," he says. "Lots of people were transporting a little bit of alcohol in those days, but Harry had these massive ships.

"I guess you had to be a little bit nuts to be successful in that business back then. Well, maybe in any business you have to be a little whacked to succeed. But this ship speaks volumes about what that man was doing. He was in it for real. He was a big-time player."

The house was undoubtedly the biggest renovation project Myslichuk has ever undertaken and he

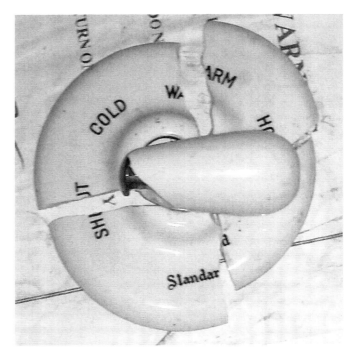

The original handle from one of the showers shattered during restoration.

says it was a project that was mentally and physically taxing. "It was non-stop, seven days a week. I'd work 12 hours at my business, then come here to the house and work some more. But it was fun at the same time. If this had happened at an earlier stage in my career, emotionally, I couldn't have undertaken it."

When he was finished, "I literally sat down on the bedroom floor and cried. It was an emotional thing because you put your heart and soul into this thing for two years. I remember thinking, 'Now what? What am I going to do now?'

"And at the same time, I know this house is a fabulous opportunity for me to show off what it is we

The master ensuite bathroom retains the original sink, toilet, body shower and tile.

The original copper eaves troughs were lost while the roof was being replaced in 2008. Normally, the hangers would fit beneath the cedar shingles, but since the new roof was in place, the hangers were modified to mount onto the soffits.

In the butler's pantry, the server cabinet was stripped down and refinished. Vern Myslichuk's son, Eric, refinishes the cabinet.

BetterMade Cabinets staff were eager to work on the project.

Vern Myslichuk intends the restored Devonshire Lodge to be a place filled with life.

do at BetterMade Cabinets. It's been fabulous for my business, and I love living here. So it's a dream come true. It can't get any better than this."

He gets a kick out of showing the place off and laughs about how he has even dragged people in off the street to take a look around. One Saturday morning he looked out the window and saw a man and woman standing outside, peering at the place, so he ran out the door and waved them over. They were visiting from the Toronto area and he said, "Come on in and take a look."

"As long as there's interest in this house, I'll always have it open. Even when it's totally – totally –

finished, with pictures on the walls and every room furnished."

Maybe that's one of the differences between Harry Low and Vern Myslichuk. Low was a more private person, guarding his family from his business affairs. He and his wife, Norah, rarely used the house for big parties. While Low was noted for extravagant parties, he nearly always held them in his expansive office, the old CP Rail station on the waterfront. Under Myslichuk's command, Devonshire Lodge has already witnessed its share of the party life.

"This is a place that's made for parties," he says. "I want this house to live again."

Vern Myslichuk shows the hole in a cement block wall that reveals a hidden room beneath the coach house.

Chapter 8:
Secrets of a Notorious Past

FOR AS LONG AS ANYONE in Windsor can recall, there have been stories of secret passageways and escape routes associated with Harry Low's old Walkerville house. One of the wilder ones had it that there was even a tunnel leading all the way to the Detroit River, where Low would, the story went, load up his ships. Given the distance, and the fact he had his own immense cargo export warehouse that sat out in public view and stretched along the river for three blocks, that seemed quite unnecessary. It was unlikely any tunnel that did exist would stretch all the way to the water.

Besides, where would they have put all that dirt?

And yet many people believed there was something there, that the house had not given up all of its mysteries.

As a young man, Paul Martin was a believer. The former prime minister and son of Liberal party legend Paul Martin Sr., says "I, too, spent a lot of time looking for Harry Low's tunnel." He laughs and adds, "Two-thirds of Windsor under the age of 20 went through the house looking for it."

Martin's wife, Sheila, grew up in the neighbourhood and was friends with her future husband's sister, Mary Anne. "Paul's sister and I spent hours down in the basement searching for it," she smiles.

During the recent renovations, owner Vern Myslichuk says countless people stopped by and told him tales of how they had gone searching the house for lost tunnels. A retired police officer recalled how he had once responded to a security alarm at the house and they had to search everywhere for possible intruders. "He swore he'd been inside a tunnel that time," says Myslichuk. "And there were rumors of a tunnel between the coach house and the main house."

So, what's really there? Are there tunnels, secret rooms, hiding places, escape hatches?

One day, a former caretaker for the property during the Martins' ownership dropped by and led Myslichuk to a spot in the basement. The blocks in the rest of the cellar were laid in the normal staggered fashion but here, in this one place, the grout lines met up. It looked as though there had been an entrance-

Above, the top of one of two giant tanks can be seen through the debris that litters the hidden room beneath the coach house.

Right, an old five-gallon Hiram Walker whisky crock sits in a corner of the hidden room.

way and it had been blocked off. Myslichuk later insulated and laid drywall over the spot, but says he still knows where it is located and some day he plans to break through and take a look.

There's another mysterious spot – this one beneath the coach house. It's reached through a trap door and then down an ancient ladder, the bottom rung of which is missing. The cellar is pitch black and you have to switch on a flashlight to find your way. If you peer straight ahead, you'll see a concrete block wall in which three or four missing blocks reveal a dark hole.

"When I saw it for the first time, I was beside myself with excitement," Myslichuk says.

Some portion of this basement had clearly been closed up long in the past and more recently, someone had begun to break through the wall. As he pointed a flashlight through the hole, Myslichuk could make out a jumble of concrete and metal, twisted and rusted. He saw the tops of two huge storage tanks and over in a corner sat a rusted jug.

(Later, Tish Harcus of the Canadian Club Brand Centre identified the jug as a five-gallon whisky storage crock invented by Hiram Walker in the late 1800s. She says the brand centre has a couple more in its possession.)

It appeared as though the blocks had been laid to cover over an old entranceway. But an entranceway to what?

Who had built the wall? Who had started to break through it?

The previous owner, Frank Vella, says it was he who broke through the block wall because just like the spot in the basement of the house, it was obvious an entranceway had been closed off. "We broke through and there was a room, maybe 10 by 10," he says, referring to the space Myslichuk also found. "Some old antique containers. We left it there and I never got back to it."

Bruce Low, grandson of Harry and Nellie Low, says that according to his grandmother, there were tunnels or storage places beneath the property where stashes of alcohol were hidden. Or perhaps the two spots – one in the cellar of the house and the other in the coach house cellar – represent opposite ends of a tunnel. An escape tunnel, perhaps? Or a hiding place? Did Harry Low believe it was a convenience for his guests, some of which endured spotty relations with the law, to have a quick escape route from the house to a waiting car?

"Yes, I believe there's something there," says Myslichuk. "Someday, I'll go looking. You can imagine what it might have been. It would be really nice to know." He pauses before adding with a smile: "But maybe not."

And what about those huge tanks? Above the tanks in the coach house basement is a drive-through garage. "You can imagine people pulling in, dropping some alcohol through a hole, into these huge tanks. Why would they do this? Were they being chased? Who knows?"

Myslichuk wonders why these portions of the two basements were closed off. Was it done by a long-ago owner who wished to keep the house's nefarious past hidden? Someone who didn't share in our modern era's fascination with uncovering Windsor's rumrunner past?

It also raises the question: Are there more of Harry Low's secrets yet to be revealed? Has Devonshire Lodge still not told us all that it knows of this fascinating era? Perhaps some day, Vern Myslichuk will be able to tell us the full story of the house he calls "the monster."

Sources:

A Note from the Author

THE EASY PART OF THIS BOOK was reporting on the work that was undertaken by Vern Myslichuk to restore Devonshire Lodge. He is here to tell his own story, which is what he has done. The more difficult part was piecing together how the house came about and what inspired it. To understand that, I needed to understand its creator, Harry Low. I needed to look back into history to find out who he was and what he did.

Not only was Harry Low not here to tell his own story, nothing is known to exist in his own words, except for the occasional brief remark reported by the news media of the day and his testimony to the Royal Commission on Customs and Excise.

Both the house and the man are steeped in legend, and legend is notoriously inaccurate. This is why, as much as possible, I have gone back to sources from the era to piece the story together and strip it of exaggeration and hearsay. Even that is a difficult path to follow.

Like the recounting of history, daily news reports are subject to interpretation, filtering, bias and, occasionally, outright lies told by the sources. Compiling the story of Devonshire Lodge and Harry Low entailed manoeuvring a minefield of supposition, rumour and purported "fact" that might not actually be true or accurate.

As I followed the trail, I was helped by many people who have provided facts, recollections, interpretations and visual materials. Vern Myslichuk and I wish to thank those who provided this invaluable information and acknowledge the following sources:

Of particular help were the descendants of Harry Low – grandson Bruce Low and nephew Gordon Low – who offered their own memories and stories recounted to them by their elders.

Others who assisted were:

John Calhoun, City of Windsor heritage planner.

Jason Grossi, architect.

Frank Vella, former Devonshire Lodge owner.

Rob Gruich, real estate agent and history buff.

Jon Kitts, Alternative Roofing.

Andrew Ledoux, Ledoux Interiors.

Haitham Rasho, Future Electric.

Lynn Baker, Architectural Conservancy of Ontario, Windsor branch.

Jim Cooper, whose father, Cyril, once owned Walkerville Lumber.

Paul Martin, Windsor Star archivist.

Paul Martin Jr., former prime minister, and his wife, Sheila Martin.

Robert Tomas, lawyer.

Marian Drouillard, City of Windsor geomatics division.

Mae Whaley, Windsor Public Library.

Robin Easterbrook, Windsor Heritage Committee member.

Norman and Beverly Marshall, and Walter Donaldson, owners of other Lawton-Bilt homes.

Evelyn McLean, former City of Windsor heritage planner.

Tish Harcus, Canadian Club Brand Centre.

Elaine Weeks, Walkerville Times and Walkerville Publishing, and author.

James Mays, author and Ford automobile enthusiast.

Other sources:

Newspapers and periodicals

Border Cities Star, Windsor Daily Star and Windsor Star, various editions from the 1920s up to 2012.

Ottawa Citizen and Montreal Gazette, various editions from 1927 to 1938.

Canadian Homes & Gardens magazine, July 1928 and February 1929.

Financial Post magazine, January 18, 1929 and June 15, 1981.

Fine Homebuilding magazine, October/November 1984.

Maclean's magazine, December 1, 1928.

Might Directories Ltd. for the city of Ottawa, various editions.

The Old-House Journal, Vol. 11, No. 3, 1983.

Vernon's city directories for Windsor and the Border Cities, various editions.

Books

Brode, Patrick. Unholy City. Windsor: Essex County Historical Society, 2013.

Fraser, Carol. Hiram Walker Remembered. Windsor: Forest Press, 1992.

Gervais, Charles Henry. The Rumrunners: A Prohibition Scrapbook. Windsor: Biblioasis, 2009.

Heron, Craig. Booze: A Distilled History. Toronto: Between the Lines, 2003.

Mingay, Jeff. One Hundred Years: A History of Essex Golf & Country Club. Windsor: Walkerville Publishing, 2002.

Schneider, Stephen. Iced: The Story of Organized Crime in Canada. Mississauga: John Wiley & Sons Canada, 2009.

Steinke, Gordon. Mobsters & Rumrunners of Canada. Edmonton: Folklore Publishing, 2003.

Websites

Ancestry website: Ancestry.com

Custom Cedar Solutions, Lakeside, Florida: Customshingles.com

Building Stories: Buildingstories.co

International Metropolis: Internationalmetropolis.com

Walkerville Times: Walkervilletimes.com

Reports

"Garden Towns, Villages and Suburbs," May 2012. Compiled for Warwick, England, District Council.

"The Low-Martin House: An Examination of its Heritage Value", by James Yanchula.

Minutes of various committees of Windsor city council.

"Seeking New Owners", a report to the Architectural Conservancy of Ontario, Pat Malicki and Nancy Morand, summer 2006.

Testimony to the Royal Commission on Customs and Excise, 1926-27, National Archives of Canada.

"Walkerville", a walking tour compiled by the city heritage planner for Windsor Architectural Conservancy Advisory Committee, 1997.

"Walkerville Study," Windsor Architectural Conservancy Advisory Committee, 1980.

Non-published material

Tom Butson, "Harry Low," April 1956 memoir, from the Windsor Star archives.

One of the items Bruce Low retains from his grandfather, Harry, is this smoking stand.

A drawing by artist Brennan M. Ware of Devonshire Lodge. (Courtesy Bruce Low)

INDEX